Bernd Wagner · Stefan Enzler (Eds.)

Material Flow Management

Improving Cost Efficiency and Environmental Performance

With 54 Figures and 16 Tables

Physica-Verlag

A Springer Company

Professor Dr. Bernd Wagner
University of Augsburg
Centre for Further Training
and Knowledge Transfer
Universitätsstraße 16
86159 Augsburg
Germany
bernd.wagner@zww.uni-augsburg.de

Dr. Stefan Enzler
imu Augsburg GmbH & Co. KG
Gratzmüllerstraße 3
86150 Augsburg
Germany
enzler@imu-augsburg.de

Editorial Assistent: Kristin Hinz, B.A.

ISSN 1860-1030
ISBN-10   3-7908-1591-8 Physica-Verlag Heidelberg New York
ISBN-13   978-3-7908-1591-7 Physica-Verlag Heidelberg New York

Cataloging-in-Publication Data applied for
Library of Congress Control Number: 2005931362

Physica is a part of Springer Science+Business Media

springeronline.com

© Physica-Verlag Heidelberg 2006
Printed in Germany

Cover-Design: Erich Kirchner, Heidelberg

SPIN 11431565   88/3153-5 4 3 2 1 0 – Printed on acid-free paper

Sustainability and Innovation

Learning Resource Centre
Tel: 01793 498381

. ⅃....ⴑ⅄ഠⴑy, Germany

Arthur P. J. Mol
Wageningen Agricultural University, The Netherlands

Sustainability and Innovation

Published Volume:

Jens Horbach (Ed.)
Indicator Systems for Sustainable Innovation
2005. ISBN 3-7908-1553-5

Preface

Material flow management gets right to the core of industrial production and its environmental impact. Basically, material flows are invariably at the nucleus of industrial production. Ecological effects are initially caused by materials: consumption and entropy of scarce resources as well as emissions resulting from the production and use of products and consumer goods.

It is only during recent years that the eco-efficient optimisation of these material flows, which aims at reducing costs while simultaneously decreasing environmental impact, has become an explicit objective of both practical and scientific activities and efforts. There has been a lot of discussion, but little has been done.

This book provides an overview of the pertinent research and scientific projects conducted between 1999 and 2005 in co-operation with industrial companies; the projects were initiated and founded by the *Bundesministerium für Bildung und Forschung* (BMBF, Federal Ministry of Education and Research).

This book illustrates the current diversity of existing operational approaches and thus also points out synergetic co-ordination options. It demonstrates the high, still unutilised potential for increasing the eco-efficiency of material flows: the long since existing, but yet unused overlapping areas between cost reduction and simultaneous environmental relief by means of efficient material utilisation. The reason for this suboptimal material flow efficiency essentially lies in the currently still low transparency of cross-departmental or cross-company material flows (with regard to the flowing physical quantities and volumes – in detail – the commercial costs/ values and flow times).

However, transparency alone is not sufficient unless there is cross-departmental and cross-company efficient communication, information exchange and co-operation between the stakeholders along the material flows.

In the end, it will be necessary to make the wide variety of isolated experiences and approaches available to a broader audience and, most of all, implement them on a more extensive basis in the companies.

The funding focus "Corporate Instruments for Sustainable Management" (INA) and this resultant publication are intended to be a step in this direction.

Augsburg, May 2005, Bernd Wagner

Contents

**4   Measuring Environmental Performance with EPM-KOMPAS
Software Tool – Material Flow Analysis, Environmental
Assessment and Success Control** 57

Edeltraud Günther, Susann Kaulich

1 Introduction

Stefan Enzler

imu augsburg GmbH & Co.KG, Augsburg/ Germany
Email: enzler@imu-augsburg.de

Within the scope of the German Federal Government's "Research for the Environment" programme, the *Bundesministerium für Bildung und Forschung* [BMBF (German Federal Ministry of Education and Research)] is funding research work on the subject of integrated environmental protection. Within this programme, various topics are compiled into funding focuses. Since 1999, the BMBF funding focus "Corporate Instruments for Sustainable Management" (INA) has bundled numerous research and development work on the following topics:

- IT tools for sustainable management
- Controlling tools for sustainable management (monetary and non-monetary assessment tools)
- Planning tools for sustainable management (operative and strategic planning tools)
- Communication tools for sustainable management.

Within these four funding fields, sustainability approaches are examined on an internal and cross-company basis, which are aligned both along value-added chains and span across the various levels of corporate function areas (such as design, work planning/ scheduling, production planning, management and control systems, accounting and controlling). Within the INA funding focus, research and development resulted in the emergence of practically-oriented concepts for integrating the requirements of sustainable management into entrepreneurial and business decision-making. The starting point for the developed solutions is the daily routine of the company as well as the current decision-making patterns of the consumers and producers. The results of the research should now contribute to fully utilising the potentials of sustainable management in the company, provide a new framework for economic research and initiate standardisation processes geared towards sustainable management.

In order to integrate the research and development tasks and moreover, enable the consideration of cross-project topics, cross-project working groups have to be organised. They represent an essential tool for effective interdisciplinary co-operation within the funding focus.

This publication summarises the results of both the "Material Flow Management and Recovery Systems" working group and the projects that were conducted. The focus of the "Material Flow Management and Recovery Systems" working group is at the core of the environmental problem: material flows and the resource consumption and emissions associated with them. The objective of the various practice-oriented projects is to reduce material related environmental pollution in conjunction with economic optimisation. To this end, new economically sound closed loop supply chain options should be taken into account for the purpose of promoting an utilisation of resources that is as intensive, sustainable and low-entropy as possible. Material flow management thus deals directly with the root of the problem, since material flows and their impact are direct causes of ecological problems. Accordingly, the reduction or substitution of material flows can directly contribute to a decrease in environmental pollution. Moreover, such changes usually result in a reduction of costs at the same time. The working group and the projects conducted concerned themselves with providing new impetuses and ideas to the dynamic structures between ecology and economy.

To present these results, this publication first describes a content-based framework on the topic of material flow management. The individual projects and their conclusions are introduced next. The conclusion then provides a comprehensive summary of the end results from the cross-project meetings as well as prospects for further possible activities.

Since the presentation of the results of the completed research projects is the main focus of this publication, a brief overview of the individual projects is provided here for informational purposes.

1.1 Brief Description of CARE Research Project

The BMBF-funded research project "CARE – Computer-Aided Resource Efficiency Accounting in Small and Medium Sized Enterprises" starts from the current state of (environmental) cost accounting and ecological information systems and takes it as a basis for developing an application method that expands the existing economic controlling systems of enterprises by adding ecological information and combines them into an integrated information system. The Resource Efficiency Accounting (REA) system, a tool developed by the Wuppertal Institute (Wuppertal, Germany), serves as the methodical framework for this. Integrating the results of the REA into corporate controlling creates a decision-making basis for Management in regards to the economic and ecological assessment and optimisation of production processes and products.

The analysis and assessment of the resource efficiency of processes and products requires lifecycle-wide data and information. Such data is available from business information systems as well as external data sources. For this, data concerning internal material and energy flows are supplemented in the form of MI values by resource consumption data from upstream and, if applicable, downstream production steps and/or the utilisation phase.

To enable more efficient use of the data for analysing internal processes and products, a standard for exchanging data between business information systems (Enterprise Resource Planning systems, ERP) and Environmental Management Information Systems (EMIS) was developed in the course of the CARE project and published in the form of a Publicly Available Specification (PAS) in co-operation with the DIN institute. In the future, this data standard will facilitate the exchange of data between the different information systems and make the data available for the economic-ecological assessment of production processes and products.

The CARE project was able to demonstrate how the systematic collection and processing of data related to internal material and energy flows as well as costs associated with them can improve the quality of company and business decisions with respect to sustainable management. The results of the basic project were tested and implemented in practice at the corporate co-operation partners: Nolte Möbel, Toshiba Europe GmbH and Muckenhaupt & Nusselt.

1.2 Brief Description of EPM-Kompas Research Project

In conjunction with the Saxon industrial partners, and by commission of the BMBF, the Professorship of Business Administration, with a particular focus on Environmental Management, at the Technische Universität (TU) Dresden *(Dresden University of Technology, Germany)* has developed, in interdisciplinary co-operation with information scientists and mechanical engineers at the TU Dresden, a tool based on the approach of integrated management of environmental and risk aspects, which can be used as both a stepping stone for introducing an environmental management system (EMS) as well as a tool for the systematic further development of an existing EMS. The free software developed in the scope of the project, EPM-KOMPAS, can be deployed for individually definable system borders (e.g. process, location, product, etc.) and supports companies in handling hazardous materials and waste, designing internal material and energy flows, setting environmental objectives, evaluating environmental protection measures and preparing reports for authorities. Along with the classic material flow analysis, also implemented are a "silent moderator" that guides users through the software as well the KOMPAS assessment (according to Günther/ Kaulich) for significant environmental aspects and ecological results breakdown.

The KOMPAS software joins the ranks of further research activities related to measuring the environmental performance of transport processes, products from the chemicals industry and products from the medical textiles sector, which are being conducted in the "Environmental Performance Measurement (EPM)" competence centre at the TU Dresden.

1.3 Brief Description of INTUS Research Project

In the "INTUS – *Operationalisation of Environmental Accounting Instruments through the Effective Use of Environmental Management Information Systems*" research project, concepts were developed for facilitating the introduction of controlling tools into the internal environmental management systems of enterprises. The new concepts relate to the three key problems with which companies are faced when striving to optimise the internal provision of information in regards to environment-oriented management. Areas to be considered here include:

- the suitability of the various environmental accounting tools;
- the provision of the tools by way of information technology (IT); and
- the organisational implementation during the introductory phase and in long-term utilisation.

In co-operation with four companies, practical solutions for the IT-aided provision of environmental performance indicators and input-output balances as well as additional information for efficient and proactive environmental protection were developed. Amongst others, an environmental performance indicator system was created and realised within SAP R/3 at Germany-based glass manufacturer SCHOTT. Experience in the medium-sized enterprise sector was gained at the Göhring company, a manufacturer of wood furniture. At Göhring, a performance indicator system was developed, and moreover, the company can now access an input-output balance directly from the Navision Financials ERP system.

The research project also examined the suitability of special software programs for modelling and analysing internal material flows. In addition, a further focus was placed on organisational issues, since it was found that the deployment of IT solutions alone is not sufficient for the successful implementation of a controlling tool.

1.4 Brief Description of IC Research Project

The basis of this contribution is the BMBF sponsored project entitled "IC – Development of an Integrated Controlling Concept Based on a Process-oriented Costing System with Regard to Optimised Material and Energy Flows in Iron, Steel and Malleable Iron Foundries" (INPROCESS). The project is an interdisciplinary research project that aims at creating practically-oriented controlling tools in a sustainable development context.

The expansion of costing systems in regards to environmental protection represents an important basis for the development of an integrated controlling concept. The approaches presented in the literature were already analysed prior to the project; both differentiating and integrating approaches were found. Within the scope of the project, a non-monetary integrated environmental activity-based costing method was developed, which records material and energy flows as well as internalised environmental costs in an integrating system and allocates them to identical reference objects. A "controlling-friendly" cost management of both environmental costs and environmental impact is only made possible by an integrated assessment of the degree to which economic and ecological objectives are achieved.

In addition to laying the theoretical foundation, the methodological approach comprises case studies examining a total of nine companies, at which individual focal tasks of the project were put into practice. The main results of this project are:

* the development of a phase model for implementing integrated controlling in foundry companies;
* the development of a model foundry;
* the preparation of industry guidelines for distributing the results; and
* an IT-aided comparison of foundry-specific software.

1.5 Brief Description of StreaM Research Project

The BMBF funded project "StreaM – Material Flow Based Closed Loop Supply Chain Management in the Electro(nics) Industry for the Purpose of Closing Material Loops" was conducted from January 2001 to April 2004 at the Technical University of Braunschweig (TU Braunschweig) by the Institute of Business Administration, Department of Production Management, in co-operation with the Institute of Machine Tools and Production Technology, Department of Product and Life Cycle Management. The Agfa-Gevaert AG (Munich/ Germany) and Electrocycling GmbH (Goslar/ Germany) companies were brought into the project as industrial partners. In light of the fact that in the future, recycling companies should be integrated into the supply chains of product manufacturers, particularly due to the requirements for expanded product responsibility, the StreaM project aims to provide information technology tools as well as strategic and operative planning tools for integrated, material flow based, cross-company supply chain management in the electronics industry, for the purpose of facilitating companies in fully utilising the resultant ecological and economic optimisation potentials. For the development of the IT tool, the concept of the recycling passport used by Agfa-Gevaert AG was applied and an Internet-based communication was platform created, taking into account the information requirement(s) arising from the various recycling options; the platform interlinked the product development phase with the post-use phase. The concept was implemented in a prototype. The developed strategic tools primarily focus on the support of long-term cross-company planning in terms of the return and re-use of product components within the scope of spare parts management. In this context, a prototype software for a strategic planning tool was developed on the basis of the "systems dynamics" simulation method. These operative planning tools comprise two main tasks:

- the development of a concept for designing business processes related to the order processing for reusing products components in spare parts management, and
- the development of a production planning, control and management system for recycling companies based on the methods of activity-based analysis and operations research.

The developed tools were validated over the course of several comprehensive case studies. Corresponding recommendations for action for the companies and for general politics were then derived from the implementation and the experience gained from the case studies.

2 Aspects of Material Flow Management

Stefan Enzler

imu augsburg GmbH & Co.KG, Augsburg/ Germany
Email: enzler@imu-augsburg.de

The term material flow management covers a broad spectrum of methods and approaches in the literature. In general, material flow management refers to the analysis and specific optimisation of material and energy flows that arise during the manufacturing of products and provision of services. Material flow management can focus on very different levels of consideration. When defining system borders for material flow management, the following areas can be specified:[1]

- Company-internal processes
- An entire company
- Supplier relationships along a value-added chain
- An entire value-added chain
- A region
- A nation.

This flexibility with respect to system borders leads us to another key topic of material flow management: the *management* of material flows. This extends beyond a merely material or technical aspect the focus lies on a system to be optimised, not an individual product or material.[2] The approach in such a systematic analysis of material flow management is the interlinking of a purely technical-economic approach (corporate input-output optimisation) with an ecological value (system) in regards to sustainability and future potentials. Successful material flow management thus also links the structural analysis of material flows with the data

---

[1] See Staudt/ Auffermann/ Schroll 2002, pp. 65 et seq.; Sterr 1998, p. 4; Wietschel 2002, p. 5; Mahammadzadeh/ Biebeler 2004, p. 10 et seq.
[2] See Marsmann 1998, p. 10

available in business information systems. A direct quantification of the quantity/ volume and costs of material flows points out the way towards new cost-cutting options.[3] Consequently, material flow management is first and foremost characterised by interdisciplinarity and networking on the basis of a normative orientation.[4] In addition to a clarification of the term, aspects of material flow management also comprise the consideration and examination of stakeholders and networks as well as the various forms of material flow management.

2.1 The Term "Material Flow Management"

In its demand for a material flow management of all material systems, the "Protection of Mankind and the Environment" Commission of Inquiry of the 12th Deutsche Bundestag (Lower House of the German Parliament) presented a quantitative and qualitative new challenge for governments, companies, science and research. At the same time, the Commission of Inquiry also provided a basic definition of the term "material flow management" from a macroeconomic standpoint:

> "Management of material flows by the involved stakeholders refers to the objective-oriented, responsible, integrated and efficient controlling of material systems, with the objectives arising from both the economic and ecological sector and with the inclusion of social aspects. The objectives are determined on a company level, within the scope of the chain in which stakeholders are involved or on a national level."[5]

Additional publications have concretised and supplemented the Commission of Inquiry's definition, e.g. by differentiating between internal and cross-company material flow management. Whereas an *internal* material flow refers to the movements of substances or materials within a company, a cross-company (*external*) material flow describes the path of a material along the value-added chain.[6] The path of cross-company material flow management is also described as the product line or product lifecycle, from the input of raw materials, manufacturing, distribution and use and consumption up to disposal.[7] Sterr defines material flow management as a "objective-oriented, structured handling of materials along the value-added

---

[3] See Enzler/ Krcmar/ Pfenning/ Scheide/ Strobel 2005, pp.63 et seq.
[4] See Brickwedde 1999, p. 13
[5] Enquete-Kommission (Commission of Inquiry) 1994, pp. 549 et seq.
[6] See Staudt et.al. 2000, p. 6
[7] See Zundel et.al. 1998, p. 319

chain, including the interests of stakeholders who are directly or indirectly involved in it"[8]. The definitions set forth by Sterr and the Commission of Inquiry clearly make the stakeholders the focus of attention within the scope of material flow management. A purely ecological and material viewpoint transforms into a stakeholder perspective that takes into account the economic concerns as well as the incentives and motivation on the part of the stakeholders.[9]

2.2 Stakeholders and Networks of Material Flow Management

2.2.1 Stakeholders in Material Flow Management

Material flow management comprises new forms of co-operation and communication as well as new organisational methods and models, since it involves the co-operation of stakeholders from a wide range of specialised disciplines and educational levels. This applies from both an internal and cross-company standpoint. However, material flow management should not only be seen from a purely stakeholder co-operation angle. Competition and conflicts also have an impact on material flow management, since they create new perspectives and decision-making structures and point out existing weak spots.[10] The primary participating stakeholders vary depending on the system borders of material flow management (internal, cross-company, regional, supraregional). Nevertheless, the success of material flow management for all stakeholders rests on the same factors: motivation and expertise as well as assertiveness and power.[11] The basic idea underlying the necessity of material flow management can be attributed to the fact that the involved material flow stakeholders cannot communicate, or cannot communicate in a objective-oriented manner, with each other and accordingly optimise the material flow without sufficient and satisfactory networking and co-ordination. As already indicated, the reasons for this can be very diverse, which explains the need for research in regards to developing methods for methods material flow management. In principle, the stakeholders involved in material flow management can be divided into two categories:[12]

---

[8] Sterr 1998, p. 3
[9] See Schneidewind 2003, p. 17
[10] See de Man/ Claus 1998, p. 72
[11] See Heck/ Knaus 2002, p. 27 and de Man/ Claus 1998, p. 73
[12] See Heck/ Knaus 2002, p. 27

- direct material flow stakeholders, and
- indirect material flow stakeholders.

The *direct* or primary stakeholders are the actual material flow managers and have a direct influence on the material flows. The *indirect* stakeholders (e.g. commercial enterprises) only indirectly impact the material flows by, e.g., setting up the general framework conditions for the respective value-added chain.[13] These two stakeholder categories can be further subdivided into five stakeholder types:[14]

1. *Economic stakeholders who directly influence material flows:* these are stakeholders who have the task of directly handling, controlling and monitoring material flows. These include, e.g., people or departments in production companies.

2. *Economic stakeholders whose decisions influence the materials-related decisions made by other stakeholders:* in this context, for example, the purchasing decisions and product ranges of commercial enterprises influence many upstream material flows. Such indirect material flow management affects the actions of the direct material flow stakeholders. Other examples of this are banks or insurance agencies.

3. *Economic stakeholders who set the framework conditions for the material flow management of a sector, industry or production chain*: this includes stakeholders who create favourable framework conditions for the direct stakeholders in material flow management, e.g., through the centralisation of information systems, providing expertise or mediating in the competitive situation between stakeholders. Such tasks are undertaken by traditionally horizontally oriented associations or by vertically organised co-operative structures.

4. *Governmental or administrative stakeholders who set the framework conditions for the material flow management of economic stakeholders (the three types described above)*: These stakeholders enable and/or promote material flow management by setting and organising relevant political framework conditions.

5. *Other stakeholders who influence the material flow management of all other stakeholders*: These include, for example, consumer organisations, environmental protection associations, standardisation institutions and other NGOs that attempt to influence the actions of all of the above-mentioned four types of stakeholders by way of their activities.

---

[13] See de Man/ Claus 1998, p. 72
[14] See de Man, R. 1994

The "Protection of Mankind and the Environment" Commission of Inquiry of the 12th Deutsche Bundestag analysed the stakeholders of material flow management. In this context, trade and industry (e.g. retailers) as well as the government were emphasised as the central stakeholders.[15] Upon a closer examination, however, the government did not directly concern itself with the management of material flows, but rather influenced the actions of the economic stakeholders by setting the political action framework. This framework includes, for example, the definition of environmental policy objectives, the specification of legal framework conditions (e.g. by means of the *Kreislaufwirtschafts- und Abfallgesetz/* German Closed Substance Cycle and Waste Management Act), the development of economic incentives as well as the collection and distribution of ecological information, public relations activities and educational policy.[16] The tasks of the government thus relate more to material policy than material flow management.[17]

According to the definition of the Commission of Inquiry, material policy and material flow policy comprises "all political measures that influence the type and extent of materials supply and usage as well as waste treatment and storage in order to secure, in the long term, the material basis of the economy in view of limited resources and the restricted pollution-bearing capacity of the environmental media"[18].

Taking this approach as a basis, a task and responsibility demarcation between the economic stakeholders and the government can be derived. With its material flow policy, the government sets up the relevant framework conditions, while the actual structure and design of material flow management, in terms of the planning, organisation, realisation, monitoring and controlling of internal and corporate material flows, is the responsibility of the trade and industry.[19]

---

[15] See Enquete-Kommission (Commission of Inquiry) 1994, pp. 591 et seq.
[16] See Henseling 2001, pp. 372 et seq.
[17] See Henseling 1998, p. 19
[18] Enquete-Kommission (Commission of Inquiry) 1994, p. 719
[19] See Mahammadzadeh/ Biebeler 2004, pp. 7 et seq.

The following diagram illustrates the distribution of tasks within the scope of material flow management:[20]

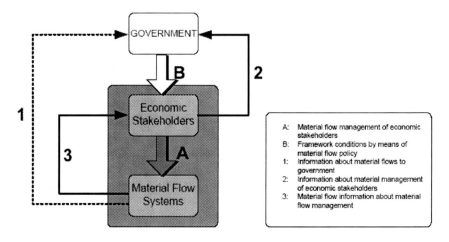

Fig. 2.1. Distribution of tasks within the scope of material flow management between economic stakeholders and the government (source: Henseling 1998, p. 19)

Schneidewind considers the possibility of the controlled management of material flows by their stakeholders and thus the existence of material flow managers to be almost fictitious. From his point of view, material flow design is a function of the close interconnection of actions, which individual stakeholders can hardly deliberately influence.[21] This underlines the complexity of this task, and points out the fact that that the stakeholders involved in material flow management and the underlying organisation are not to be seen as purely rational, constantly co-operative, unbiased information processing machines; their corresponding vested interests also play a role. Accordingly, the development of a homogeneous perception of material flows and information flows is one of the central tasks of material flow management; only then can stakeholders design material flows in a co-ordinated and objective-oriented manner.[22] The inclusion of the various stakeholders in the shared conception and visualisation of material flows can create a uniform perspective, a uniform language as well as an inte-

---

[20] See Henseling 1998, p. 19
[21] See Schneidewind 2003, pp. 17 et seq.
[22] See imu augsburg GmbH&Co.KG/ Zentrum für Weiterbildung und Wissenstransfer, Universität Augsburg (Centre for Further Training and Knowledge Transfer, University of Augsburg/ Germany) 2003, pp. 4 et seq.

grated concept of material flow management.[23] After examining individual stakeholders along with their responsibilities and task areas, a potential co-operation form of material flow management has to be analysed next. The direct influence sphere of an individual stakeholder involved in a material flow management rarely extends beyond one or two links of the value-added chain. Usually, there is no direct causality between the activities of a raw material producer and a recycler.

Since company co-operations that span across many links of the value-added chain are generally the exception, material flow management in practice concerns specific areas of the networked material flows and stakeholder relationships.[24] De Man has derived the following "rules" from extensive experience with actual material flow oriented co-operations in practice:[25]

- Cross-stakeholder and shared analysis and visualisation of the material flows to be designed
- Objective-oriented communication about the material flows to be designed
- Definition of realistic ecological objectives with the explicit inclusion of economic goals
- Realistic assessment of the enterprise's own role
- The aim for forms of co-operation that are compatible with the econo-mic reality
- Gradual and systematic implementation of material flow management
- Assurance that the decision-maker(s) of a material flow management are provided with action-relevant information concerning the quantities/ volumes and values of the material flows.

2.2.2 Vertical and Horizontal Co-operations in Material Flow Management (Networking)

Co-operations in material flow management are formed for a variety of reasons. The motivation for co-operations arises from the following rea-sons or a combination thereof:[26]

- Personal commitment and company culture
- Experience in environmental (protection) management

---

[23] See Strobel, van Riesen, Berger 2002, pp. 84 et seq.
[24] See de Man/ Haralabopoulou/ Henseling 1998, p. 24
[25] See de Man 1999, pp. 64 et seq. and Strobel/ Müller 2003, pp. 122 et seq.
[26] See de Man/ Haralabopoulou/ Henseling 1998, pp. 21 et seq.

- Economic benefits
- Demand for environmentally-friendly products
- Environment related quality assurance
- Public pressure
- Economic incentives
- "Green" or "Eco" labels/ seals
- Legal environmental regulations.

Co-operations in the form of product lines or value-added chains are frequently very simply described as an overview of linear, consecutive steps. However, such descriptive chain models are far from reality. For the most part, complex products are manufactured from parts, which in turn are produced in their own value-added chains. The same applies to the utilisation and disposal phases, which are intertwined with various segments of the value-added chains. Thus, the basis is then a value-added network rather than a value-added chain.[27]

Vertical Co-operations

The emergence of vertical co-operations is primarily rooted in optimisation potentials that arise from network-internal co-ordination. This includes co-operations between raw material suppliers, manufacturers, users, recyclers and waste disposal companies.

The following are examples of vertical co-operations:[28]

- Development of redistribution solutions with downstream material flow stages as a result of take back obligations
- Co-ordination of assembly and disassembly methods
- Optimisation of purchaser production processes by manufacturers (in this context, the scope spans up to the acceptance of responsibility for subprocesses, environmental regulations and risks of the purchaser).
- Working group for resolving technical problems related to the cross closed loop supply chain of materials.

Horizontal Co-operations

Horizontal co-operations arise if risks related to individual materials can no longer be directly attributed to a responsible party. This responsibility can then be undertaken on the horizontal co-operation level. Analogous to this, horizontal co-operations can also emerge if solutions within the scope

---

[27] See de Man/ Claus 1998, p. 73
[28] See Staudt/ Auffermann/ Schroll 2002, p. 66

of material flow management cannot be achieved with the means of an individual enterprise. It is only by bundling the capabilities of several stakeholders that an economic and technically efficient material flow management can be achieved.[29]

The following are examples of horizontal co-operations:[30]

- Agreement between the involved stakeholders in regards to the "paper" material flow, in which the stakeholders agree not to use certain types of printing ink which are problematic in terms of recycling (such co-operations only prove successful if all printing companies stick to the agreement, which demonstrates the complementary effect of horizontal and vertical material flow management measures).
- Impact of a material or occurring environmental problem cannot be directly attributed to a responsible party, therefore, countermeasures can only be effectively implemented on the level of industry or other horizontal co-operations (e.g. opting out of CFC production, or the usage of recycled paper in the paper industry).
- A lack of technical or economic capacities on the individual company level can lead to horizontal co-operations; waste and disposal associations exist here on the industry level (e.g. in the automotive industry)[31] or regional level (e.g. the Heidelberg Pfaffengrund industrial area)[32].

2.3 Forms of Material Flow Management

Company co-operations that span across many links of the value-added chain are rather rare. Various forms of material flow management arise depending on the motivation of the co-operation and the specific characteristics of the material flows in a value-added chain. In practice, due to the recurring patterns, these networked material flows and stakeholder networks can be divided into the following areas.[33]

---

[29] See de Man/ Claus 1998, p. 74
[30] See Staudt/ Auffermann/ Schroll 2002, p. 67
[31] See Hansen/ Meyer/ Nagel 1998, p. 19
[32] See Sterr 1998
[33] See de Man et. al. 1997

2.3.1 Ecological Quality Improvement and Quality Assurance

This form of material flow management only requires a minor amount of co-operation between the stakeholders. It is primarily geared towards eco-logical modernisation by means of the deliberate selection of environmentally-friendly materials and consumables. The driving force is either the manufacturer itself or the retailers (e.g. trade and industry), which put pressure on the preliminary suppliers to comply with quality requirements pertaining to materials and products.

2.3.2 Material Flow Related Service and Responsibility

The central stakeholder in this form of material flow management is the company that markets the substances, preparations or materials and thus optimally assists the stakeholders of the downstream chain in the best way to handle those substances, preparations and materials. This type of service includes, e.g., labelling, directions for use, professional consulting and support in optimising the respective production processes. Furthermore, the tasks of the "marketers" may also include the responsibility for the subprocesses or environmental regulations and risks of the downstream stakeholders.

2.3.3 Lifecycle Based Product Optimisation

In lifecycle based product optimisation, manufacturers attempt to eco-logically optimise their products across the entire lifecycle. This form of co-operation extends beyond merely issuing guidelines to preliminary suppliers in regards to quality requirements. The product optimisation takes place in co-operation with the stakeholders involved in upstream and downstream stages of the value-added chain. In this context, production system suppliers and logistics companies can also take on an important role. On the whole, this form is best facilitated by a close co-operation between manufacturers, suppliers, retailers, users and disposal companies.

2.3.4 Product-related Recycling and Disposal

In this form, the focus is on the co-operation between manufacturers, disposal companies and recyclers. The manufacturer organises the optimal utilisation, recycling and disposal of its product(s) by optimising the product design and entering into a close co-operation with recycling and disposal company stakeholders. Within the scope of the co-operation, the manufacturer provides for the necessary information and a suitable infrastructure.

2.4 Summary

The various aspects of material flow management demonstrate the possibilities, opportunities and broad application spectrum offered by this approach. In the previous sections, the current state of knowledge has been comprehensively and clearly summarised by examining material flow management from different perspectives.

Since the methods for material flow management can be best illustrated with project examples, the latest approaches and developments will be described in the following by means of research and implementation projects that have already been conducted.

The thorough analysis of material flow management indicates that there are still hurdles blocking the widespread application of material flow management in corporate practice. In order to further level out the path for promising innovations based on this valuable approach, this book concludes with an examination of the outlook and perspectives of still pending developments of material flow management. Since with consistent further development, this approach promises to make an important contribution to sustainable development in our society.

References

Brickwedde F (1999) Stoffstrommanagement – Herausforderung für eine nachhaltige Entwicklung. 4th International Summer Academy St. Marienthal. Osnabrück

De Man R (1994) Erfassung von Stoffströmen aus naturwissenschaftlicher und wirtschaftswissenschaftlicher Sicht – Akteure, Entscheidungen und Informationen im Stoffstrommanagement. In: Enquete-Kommission (*Commission of Inquiry*) (ed) „Schutz der Menschen und der Umwelt": Umweltverträgliches Stoffstrommanagement – Konzepte, Instrumente, Bewertung. vol 1. Bonn

De Man R, Claus F, Völkle E, Ankele K, Fichter K (1997) Aufgaben des betrieblichen und betriebsübergreifenden Stoffstrommanagements. Umweltbundesamt-Texte 11 (*German Federal Environment Office Text 11*). Berlin

De Man R, Claus F (1998) Kooperationen, Organisationsformen und Akteure. In: Friege, Engelhardt, Henseling (eds) Das Management von Stoffströmen. Geteilte Verantwortung – Nutzen für alle. Berlin Heidelberg

De Man R, Haralabopoulou D, Henseling K-O (1998) Ziele, Anlässe und Formen des Stoffstrommanagements. In: Friege, Engelhardt, Henseling (eds) Das Management von Stoffströmen. Geteilte Verantwortung – Nutzen für alle. Berlin Heidelberg

Enquete-Kommission „Schutz des Menschen und der Umwelt" des 12. Deutschen Bundestags (ed) (*Commission of Inquiry of the 12th German Bundestag*) (1994) Die Industriegesellschaft gestalten – Perspektiven für einen nachhaltigen Umgang mit Stoff- und Materialströmen. Bonn

Enzler S, Krcmar H, Pfennig R, Scheide W, Strobel M (2005) Eco-Efficient Controlling of Material Flows with Flow Cost Accounting: ERP-Based Solutions of the ECO Rapid Project. In: Hilty L, Seifert E, Treibert R (eds) (2005) Information Systems for Sustainable Development. Hershey

Hansen U, Meyer P, Nagel C (1998) Entsorgungslogistische Netzwerke. In: Umweltwirtschaftsforum. Edition 6, vol 2, pp 16 - 20

Heck P, Knaus M (2002) Akteure und Netzwerke im Stoffstrommanagement. In: Heck P, Bemmann U (eds) Praxishandbuch Stoffstrommanagement 2002/ 2003. Strategien – Umsetzung – Anwendung in Unternehmen/ Kommunen/ Behörden. Cologne

Henseling K-O (1998) Grundlagen des Managements von Stoffströmen. In: Friege, Engelhardt, Henseling (eds) Das Management von Stoffströmen. Geteilte Verantwortung – Nutzen für alle. Berlin Heidelberg

Henseling K-O (2001) Stoffstrommanagement. In: Schulz F et.al. (eds) Lexikon Nachhaltiges Wirtschaften. Munich Vienna, pp 369 – 373

imu augsburg GmbH&Co.KG, Zentrum für Weiterbildung und Wissenstransfer Universität Augsburg (*Centre for Further Training and Knowledge Transfer, University of Augsburg/ Germany*) (eds) (2003) Flussmanagement für Produktionsunternehmen. Material- und Informationsflüsse nachhaltig gestalten. Frankfurt

Mahammadzadeh M, Biebeler H (2004) Stoffstrommanagement. Grundlagen und Beispiele. Schriftenreihe des Instituts der deutschen Wirtschaft (*Series by Institute of Germany Economy*) 1/2004. Cologne

Marsmann M (1998) Von der Problembeschreibung zur Problemlösung: Konzepte und Wege eines modernen Umweltmanagements für Produkte. In: Friege, Engelhardt, Henseling (eds) Das Management von Stoffströmen. Geteilte Verantwortung – Nutzen für alle. Berlin Heidelberg

Schneidewind U (2003) „Symbole und Substanzen" – ein alternativer Blick auf das Management von Wertschöpfungsketten und Stoffströmen. In: Schneidewind U, Goldbach M, Fischer D, Seuring S (eds) Symbole und Substanzen. Perspektiven eines interpretativen Stoffstrommanagements. Marburg

Staudt E, Auffermann S, Schroll M (2002) Zur Umsetzbarkeit einzel- und überbetrieblichen Stoffstrommanagements. In: Heck P, Bemmann U (eds) Praxishandbuch Stoffstrommanagement 2002/ 2003. Strategien – Umsetzung – Anwendung in Unternehmen/ Kommunen/ Behörden. Cologne

Staudt E, Schroll M, Schwering M (2000) Praxisleitfaden Stoffstrommanagement. Ein Wegweiser zur Optimierung von Material- und Energieströmen. In: Staudt E (ed) Berichte aus der angewandten Innovationsforschung. no 189 (*Report from Applied Innovation Research. no 189*). Bochum

Sterr T (1998) Aufbau eines zwischenbetrieblichen Stoffverwertungsnetzwerks im Heidelberger Industriegebiet Pfaffengrund. Heidelberg

Strobel M (2001) Systemisches Flussmanagement. Flussorientierte Kommunikation für eine ökologische und ökonomische Unternehmensentwicklung. Augsburg

Strobel M, Müller U (2003) Flusskostenrechnung – Ein ERP-basiertes Instrument zur systematischen Reduzierung des Materialeinsatzes. In: Tschandl M, Posch A (eds) Integriertes Umweltcontrolling. Von der Stoffstromanalyse zum integrierten Bewertungs- und Informationssystem. Wiesbaden

Strobel M, Van Riesen S, Berger M (2002) Nachhaltigkeitsmanagement durch Flussmanagement. In: BUND/ UnternehmensGrün (eds) Zukunftsfähige Unternehmen. Wege zur nachhaltigen Wirtschaftsweise von Unternehmen. Munich

Wietschel M (2002) Stoffstrommanagement. Frankfurt/ Main

Zundel S, Bunke D, Schramm E, Steinfeld M (1998) Stoffstrommanagement. Zwischenbilanz einer Diskussion In: ZfU – Zeitschrift für Umweltschutz & Umweltrecht, Edition 21, vol 3, pp 317 - 339

3 Computer Aided Resource Efficiency Accounting

Timo Busch, Severin Beucker, Andreas Müller

Timo Busch, Wuppertal Institute for Climate, Environment, Energy, Sustainable Production and Consumption, Germany
Email: timo.busch@wupperinst.org

Severin Beucker, Institute for Human Factors and Technology Management (IAT), University of Stuttgart, Germany
Email: severin.beucker@iat.uni-stuttgart.de

Andreas Müller, TOSHIBA Europe GmbH, Regensburg Operations, Germany
Email: Andres.mueller@toshiba-tro.de

3.1 Introduction

Resource Efficiency Accounting (REA) is a method developed by the Wuppertal Institute (Wuppertal, Germany) aiming at the lifecycle-wide ecological assessment of processes and products. The scope of the project CARE[1] (Computer Aided Resource Efficiency Accounting) was to develop an application method basing on the REA, which expands the existing economic controlling systems of enterprises by adding ecological information concerning environmental impacts. The innovative approach of the project is to supplement tools already deployed in the course of environmental and material flow accounting with ecological lifecycle data and ensure an efficient assessment process by the use of software and information technology. In the three-year-long project, the Wuppertal Institute, University of Stuttgart Institute for Human Factors and Techno-

---

[1] The project CARE is a joint research project funded by the Bundesministerium für Bildung und Forschung (BMBF, Federal Ministry of Education and Research, Fördernummer/ Reference No: 01 RU 0016/17).

logy Management (Stuttgart, Germany) and the Ingenieurbüro synergitec (engineering consultants) established the scientific basis. The central task was to demonstrate how flow cost based material and energy flow concepts can be expanded by a lifecycle perspective and how the associated data collection and generation process can be supported by the use of information technology (IT). At the same time the results were implemented and subjected to practical application tests on-site at the corporate partners: Nolte Möbel (furniture), Toshiba Europe (notebooks) and Muckenhaupt & Nusselt (special cables). The objective of these implementation projects was to integrate the economic-ecological assessment approach into already existing controlling systems at the participating companies. The integration should thus create a new basis for corporate decision-making aiming at the optimisation of material and energy flows as well as cost flows.

In the following sections, the motivation and conceptual design of the project will be presented; chapter 3.2 will then provide an in-depth description of the assessment methodology. Chapter 3.3 will finally describe the practical application oth the methodology.

3.1.1 Background

As a result of the opening of European internal markets, growing globalisation and the current economic development in Germany, enterprises are faced with increasingly intensified competitive pressure. As a response to these challenges, streamlining and rationalisation has prevailed in recent years, with workforce as the major cost factor frequently taking the spotlight. Other cost blocks are often disregarded, even if their share of the total costs is at least as high. Thus, considerable opportunities are overlooked that could financially relieve companies while modernising them at the same time. The question to be asked here is why efficiency aspects extending beyond the economies of scale and personnel costs play only a subordinate role in enterprises.

Experiences in recent years have clearly shown that a very high potential for reducing costs and improving the competitiveness of companies lies in increasing material efficiency. In a typical cost distribution of a manufacturing company, approx. 60 % of costs are attributed to materials, while e.g. only 25 % are ascribed to personnel.[2]

---

[2] See Bundesumweltministerium/ Umweltbundesamt (Federal Ministry for the Environment/ Federal Environmental Agency) (2001, p. 526)

Materials are thus the central factor for manufacturers and as such, have a direct effect on competitiveness. It can be stated that the associated saving potentials are not fully exploited in most enterprises. Accordingly, the costs of material and energy usage are frequently underestimated and cost-cutting is primarily equated with reductions in personnel costs while productivity is equated with work productivity.

Increasing material efficiency can lead to more added value, with a simultaneous reduction in the consumption of natural resources. According to the empirical findings of the management consulting company Arthur D. Little, increasing material efficiency can cut production costs by 20% in almost every case.[3]

3.1.2 Macroeconomic Objective Definition

The World Business Council for Sustainable Development has defined the objective for macroeconomic growth as the production of useable goods and services in conjunction with a continuously decreasing consumption of natural resources. To put it the other way around, creating as much prosperity as possible with a given amount of resources is one of the most important prerequisites for a sustainable economic system.[4] Such an integrated approach to resource consumption and costs can be described as "eco-efficiency"[5].

Material flows constitute an essential element for measuring eco-efficiency on the macro level. In this context, all material flows produced and initiated by a society are examined, from the exploitation of raw materials to the processing and use of products up to waste disposal. They form the physical basis of the economy and at the same time trigger a vast range of environmental changes. For measurability purposes, the Total Material Requirement (TMR) indicator is a suitable scale. It determines the total material consumption of an economy, including the "ecological rucksacks" associated with the respective material flows, that is to say all the total consumption and expenditures needed for the provision of materials.[6] For that reason not only the domestic material inputs are taken into account, but also material movements and consumption in foreign countries. Such movements and consumptions can derive from inputs required for producing the imported preliminary work, services and goods.

---

[3] See Fischer et al. 2004, p. 247
[4] See articles in Weizsäcker et al. 2004
[5] See Schaltegger/ Sturm 1990
[6] See Bartelmus et al. 2001

The consideration of the total quantity of moved and consumed materials is also called a "lifecycle perspective".

The relationship between the economic performance (e.g. gross domestic product) and the TMR of an economy is described by means of the material productivity. In the macroeconomic dimension, an improvement in eco-efficiency means an increase in material productivity.

An absolute decoupling of the economic performance from the consumption of natural resources can be stated as a declared objective by every economy following a sustainability perspective. Sustainable development, in both the ecological and economic dimension, can only be achieved if economic growth does not lead to a real rise in the consumption of natural. Otherwise rebound effects would counteract any eco-efficiency progress. Since the beginning of the 1990s, environmental policy has been strongly promoting more and more preventive environmental protection measures – be it the United Nation's "Cleaner Production" programme (UNEP), the "Eco-efficiency Initiative" of the World Business Council for Sustainable Development (WBCSD) or the individual environmental protection plans instituted by various nations (e.g. Austrian Federal Government, 1996; BMU (German Federal Ministry for the Environment, Nature Conservation and Nuclear Safety), 1998). However, according to the third report of the European Environment Agency, this decoupling has not occurred to a sufficient extent yet.[7]

The microeconomic level plays a decisive role in the realisation of the macroeconomic objective: managers and CEO's have to recognise that the relevant "adjusting screws" lie in their own enterprises. Eco-efficiency can in this case be defined as a strategic guide rail for business decisions and planning. In the sense of a bottom-up-approach, this is an important prerequisite for eliminating the macro-societal rebound effects.

3.1.3 Eco-efficiency as a Strategic "Guide Rail" for Enterprises

The implementation of eco-efficiency options on the micro or company level assume that managers and stakeholders realise an inherent benefit in the implementation of the options, adopt this principle and implement it with concrete strategies and measures. An examination of company practice demonstrates that eco-efficiency is relevant for decision-making, if specific optimisation projects can show clear cost saving potentials. The most practical approach therefore lies in focusing on the internal material

---

[7] See European Environment Agency 2003

and energy flows. The efficient use of resources thus becomes a determining factor with respect to the competitiveness of the company.

For the application-oriented research, the question to be addressed is how this interrelationship can be represented in a feasible and operationally implementable manner on both an internal and cross-company level. This means that enterprises require methods and tools to facilitate them in determining the most efficient utilisation of resources and presenting the resulting benefits.

The following factors are crucial to the practicability and operationability of the methods and tools: (1) the processes for measuring, presenting and visualising resource efficiency have to ensure that the expenses and effort associated with the data collection and processing are kept as low as possible. This proves especially difficult if significant results are desired, i.e. the effectiveness of the indicators should be maintained. The needs of small and medium sized enterprises are frequently not met by complex assessment procedures, or the required personnel and financial means are not sufficiently available. As the first key requirement, methods and tools should therefore utilise existing data sources and data collection systems and be compatible with the company's existing systems and processes. (2) Furthermore, the mapping of the results is a crucial success factor. Extensive data and information concerning potential cost and success factors generally have to be taken into consideration when making decisions concerning rationalisation, streamlining and investments. But multidimensional results matrices on ecological consequences and detailed improvement options are less informative. Instead, ecological information on processes and products should be prepared and presented in a compact form that supplies easily understandable and significant supplementary information in addition to the already existing criteria. This allows the management of a company to use the information as an operational basis for decision making on process design. Such information can also support strategic business decisions, e.g. during the product planning process, and thus contribute to securing the medium- and long-term success of a company.

3.1.4 Data Diversity and Decision Support Systems

A multitude of data and information is needed for the economical and ecological assessment in enterprises. In manufacturing companies, sources for such data and information can be business information systems, such as Enterprise Resource Planning (ERP) systems or Plant Data Collection (PDC) systems. In such systems, information relevant to the company's cost and material flows are collected, processed and stored; this data can be used for assessing the resource efficiency of the enterprise.[8]

An important source for evaluating environmentally relevant factors and costs is the master data pertaining to, e.g., production planning and controlling (also see Section 3.2.5):

- The article master contains information on end products, assemblies and components, and may also include production and process materials.
- Bills of material depict the component composition of products.
- Activity charts describe production processes. An activity chart contains a description of the transformation of workpieces from the raw state into the manufactured state.
- The operating resources master data contains all the basic data about the individual operating resources and equipment. Operating resources and equipment comprise all the resources required for production, such as tools, machines and personnel. They are relevant insofar as that operating resources and equipment are substantial consumers in a production process.

The list shows that the use of company data plays an important role in assessing the resource efficiency of a company. If the available material flow and cost data are successfully utilised, the process of generating results within the scope of economical and ecological assessment can be much more efficiently designed. In contrast, business information systems do not include data for estimating the environmental impacts of companies' activities. For an effective assessment, ecological impact data needs to be linked with the information on material flows using existing indicators and impact assessment processes. To this end, the goal of the project CARE was to test, in practice, the suitability of the MIPS (Material Input per Service Unit, see Section 3.2.3) concept and the corresponding material intensity values for the purpose of assessing environmental impacts. In addition to the aforementioned business information systems, Environmental Management Information Systems (EMIS) represent a different, specific group of IT systems that can be used for assessing material flow related data under costs and environmental restraints. Hence, the project CARE examined the different options of using EMIS in combination with business information systems for the assessment of internal processes. A major outcome of this work is a Publicly Available

---

[8] Also see the results report from work package KP2.2 "ERP Systems and their Data Pool for Resource Efficiency Accounting" at
http://www.oekoeffizienz.de/care/

Specification (PAS 1025)[9] for the exchange of environmentally relevant data between ERP systems and EMIS.

The PAS constitutes a standardisation in the form of a prenorm, which can be used at a later point in time e.g. for creating a DIN ISO standard. It was developed in co-operation with the Fraunhofer-Institut für Arbeitswirtschaft und Organisation IAO (Fraunhofer Institute for Industrial Engineering) and the companies: infor business solutions AG, TechniDataAG and ifu - Institut für Umweltinformatik Hamburg GmbH (Institute for Environmental Infomatics Hamburg GmbH).

The PAS describes an interface specification that enables the transfer of master data and any available movement data from ERP systems to an EMIS. Particularly for material flow management, such data is an important basis for conducting environmental impact assessments. The PAS 1025 thus represents an initial approach for the cross-system, standardised exchange of environmentally relevant data.

3.2 Methodological Approach

Based on the factors practicability and operation ability, a specific approach for implementing an IT-supported REA was developed in the project. This section describes the underlying approach of Resource Efficiency Accounting and presents the methodological approach for a practical enterprise-based application.

3.2.1 Definition and Limitations of Resource Efficiency Accounting

The efficient use of operating resources (in the sense of material and energy) pursues two fundamental objectives: on one hand, the internal activities related to the consumption of natural resources should be optimised, and on the other hand, associated costs should be reduced. The simultaneous consideration of these two objectives in conjunction with a continual improvement process is the task of Resource Efficiency Accounting. REA can therefore be seen as a decision supporting system for the enterprise. Data concerning internal material and energy flows and

---

[9] A PAS is a German prenorm, published by the German Institute for Standardization. The PAS 1025 can be obtained from the Beuth Verlag publishing house/ Deutschen Institut für Normung (DIN/ German Institute for Standardization)

costs involved therein is systematically collected, prepared and integrated into the existing internal decision-making process. Thus, the REA concept does not represent a new cost accounting system. The underlying cost concept comprises purchasing and procurement costs, production-related flow costs as well as the internal environmental costs.[10] The REA methodological approach aimes to expand environmental activity-based costing by adding material and energy flow information as well as ecologically relevant data from the pre-production chains. It therefore meets the criteria for an effective method tool, since lifecycle-wide data on ecological aspects are included via the mapping of pre-production chains. Accordingly, REA provides the starting point for expanding the cost accounting by adding the externalised environmental effects caused by enterprises.[11] However, this internationalisation takes place via the integration of ecological data and not through the extensive, costly and controversially discussed monetarisation of external effects.[12] Likewise, the lifecycle perspective is limited to ecological aspects. For the relatively complex procedure in the economic dimension refer to the approaches addressed by Fassbender-Wyands (2001) and Seuring (2001).

In mapping the objective function as a two-dimensional system with an integrated lifecycle perspective, REA differs significantly from existing environmental costs and process cost accounting methods.[13] First, it is based on material and energy flow optimisation concepts.[14] This applies to both the cost and material flow dimensions. In particular, the analysis of material and energy flows, i.e. knowledge of the temporal and locational distribution of deployed materials and energies in the course of the production, is an essential premise for being able to dynamically influence processes. To ensure further allocation of the material and energy data, all volumes/ quantities are recorded in weight units. In a second step, additional information on the lifecycle-wide ecological impacts is added.

Due to its orientation on internal material flows, REA can be practically and efficiently supported by business information systems as well as EMIS

---

[10] This definition of environmental costs is based on the systematic developed by Faßbender-Wynands 2001, p. 16. Due to the monetarisation issue, non-relevant microeconomic costs (costs of external effects) are not taken into consideration.

[11] See Schulz et al. 2000, p. 21

[12] See Busch/ Orbach 2003

[13] For a definition of environmental activity-based costing, see Letmathe/ Wagner 2002; for a comparison of the individual concepts, see Heupel/ Wendisch 2002, p. 3

[14] See Strobel/ Redmann 2002; Hockerts et al. 1999; Strobel/ Wagner 1997; Fischer/ Blasius 1995

(see Section 3.1.4). This can be realised on the basis of existing business information systems or in combination with EMIS. In particular, the environmental impact assessment step can be designed in an efficient manner by utilising the publicly available material intensity values for assessing the environmental impact.

3.2.2 Economic Dimension – Process Cost Accounting

The economic dimension of the REA takes data into consideration that is relevant for assessing the economic feasibility of decisions. This is primarily cost and activity accounting and the business accounting data. On principle, the economic dimension can be based on a company's existing cost accounting. However, the introduction of the REA presents itself an opportunity to conduct a critical analysis of the existing cost accounting allocation keys.

Mainly, material and energy consumption costs are often allocated to cost centres and cost units with low precision. This leads to distorting information on the actual cost distribution in a company.

The weak spots of traditional cost and activity accounting with respect to the provision of business information on eco-efficiency potentials are known and have been intensively discussed in the literature.[15] The causes for the limited expressiveness are considered to be lack of transparency in regards to (1) the company's process structures, (2) the company's cost structure, (3) the temporal structure of the cost incurrence and allocation as well as (4) the specific cost elements and structures.[16] To support decisions concerning this, conventional cost accounting systems were further developed and refined. In particular, process cost accounting is based on the concept that the activities of a company are categorised into processes and that operational procedures regarding material and energy flows, including their corresponding costs, are made transparent.[17] Process accounting is therefore especially well-suited as the basis of the economic approach of REA. Nevertheless, since there are expenses and efforts inherent in the process, it is only recommended for small enterprises to a limited extent.[18] Use of the REA is also possible within the scope of other

---

[15] See e.g. Jasch 2001, p. 18; Remer 1997, p. 25 et seq.
[16] See Seuring 2001
[17] For a more detailed description of this, see Wagner/ Strobel 2003 as well as the Landesanstalt für Umweltschutz (State Institute for Environmental Protection) Baden-Württemberg 2000.
[18] See Loew 2001, p. 11

cost accounting systems, but crucial potentials can then easily be overlooked or are harder to identify.

3.2.3 Ecological Dimension – Material Intensity

In addition to economic information, REA provides company decision-makers with data concerning the ecological effects of their actions. The assessment data used in the REA is based on company internal material and energy flows. By means of a precise retracing of the internal material and energy flows, each process or product can be allocated to a specific, internal consumption. However, an assessment of the eco-effectiveness and eco-efficiency, two key factors in determining the "overall corporate sustainability"[19], based on this type of information is limited in scope. The outcome of internal flow analysis only enables a one-sided assessment of the ecological dimensions: If the outcome of a process optimisation or material substitution entails a reduced consumption of the respective material or energy, this is considered an ecological improvement. But beyond this, the method does not facilitate assessments and comparisons concerning various input factors (substances, materials and energy forms).

Moreover the issue of interdependencies and the complexity of ecological relationships also have to be taken into account: if material flow A is able to be reduced, how will material and energy flows B-Z react? Supposing other internal material flows are increased this way, how can it be assessed, in the course of an overall analysis, as to whether the ecological performance – allowing for all internal material and energy flows – improves or rather deteriorates? Furthermore, only examining internal effects, does not correspond to the concept of global sustainable development. Taken to the extreme, this would mean that a company outsources all procedures and processes not considered effective and efficient in terms of ecological aspects and subsequently presents itself as an ecologically successfully enterprise. For this reason, assessments and optimisations of ecological effectiveness and efficiency should always take into account the lifecycle-wide effects. I.e. the ecological effects of upstream and downstream processes have to be included in decisions. This affects the entire value-added chain as well as the using stage.

But how then can the aforementioned ecological interdependencies be recorded and mapped without counteracting or violating the factors and conditions previously described as essential to the practicability and operation ability of business tools? To this end, the data collected over the

---

[19] Dyllick/ Hockerts 2002

course of the material and energy flow analysis is linked with their respective material intensity value.[20] The inclusion of material intensities has three fundamental advantages: (1) Information on the ecological effectiveness can be derived from the results, since the material intensities describe the lifecycle-wide resource consumption of materials, energy and transports. (2) Complexity is significantly reduced, since results are represented as physical quantities. This enables a comparison of the different alternatives and substitutes, while also allowing a summation of different values of internal consumption forms. (3) Material intensity values do not have to be individually collected: they are provided for many substances and materials.[21]

For the purpose of determining the resource efficiency in the scope of internal assessment procedures, the material intensities are collected using the Total Material Requirement (TMR) defined on the macro level. The TMR value is based on the MIPS concept. MIPS stands for Material Input Per Service Unit.[22]

MIPS consists of two components, the Material Input (MI) and the Service unit (S). The material input comprises all materials primarily taken from or moved through nature, which are required on a system-wide basis, i.e. for production, demand and disposal processes. The determined material inputs are subdivided into five input categories; the unit of measurement is the mass in kg or t. The five input categories are: abiotic (non-renewable) raw materials, biotic (renewable) raw materials, soil/ground transport, water and air.

The TMR value sums up the first three categories, thus providing information about all material intakes, consumption and movements in the global environment. These inputs in the technosphere are called material inputs. The two categories water and air are not taken into account, since they usually do not contribute to new findings in terms of business optimisation decisions. In cases where this does not apply (e.g. when assessing the water conservation potentials in cleaning processes), these aspects can be separately taken into consideration.

The concept does not include output aspects; accordingly, resulting external effects and their damage potential are not mapped. This is certainly a weak spot if the claim of a comprehensive and all-embracing

---

[20] In this context, material intensity values are described as physical quantities (e.g. in kilograms or tons), see Ritthof et al. 2003, and not, as is the case e.g. with input-output analysis, in the form of monetary indicators; for more on the latter, see Wiehle et al. 2003, p. 49.

[21] See Wuppertal Institut 2003

[22] See Schmidt-Bleek 2004 and Schmidt-Bleek 1994

assessment is being pursued. However, to be noted here are three essential factors that nevertheless speak in favour of the approach of material intensities for ecological assessments: (1) scientifically, there is no definitive clarification regarding the way in which a comprehensive and all-embracing assessment can take place. This particularly applies to collection and evaluation approaches, e.g. in order to determine and compare different toxicity levels of substances or products. (2) A corresponding analysis and assessment is extremely time-consuming and costly, and would require a multidimensional results matrix. Consequently, this method is less suitable for application-oriented, practical processes. (3) To a certain extent, the output quantities not explicitly included are indirectly recorded via the input approach: all materials that are emitted or separated during the production process are first recorded and assessed as inputs.

3.2.4 Eco-efficiency: Objective Function

The objective of the REA is the simultaneous examination of economic and ecological aspects. As an objective function, REA hence defines both an economic and ecological dimension; both dimensions are mapped in a resource efficiency portfolio, thus permitting a differentiated analysis of processes and products. Therefore, one can differentiate between:

- an eco-efficient objective function,
- cost-efficient business strategies,
- resource-efficient business strategies, and
- ecologically-economically less relevant areas.

The REA can thus include individual operating processes as well as end products. In both cases, the objective of the portfolio is to provide Management with a decision-making basis for relative comparisons of two or more product or process alternatives. The individual axes of the portfolios are described by the material and energy flow based cost data (X-axis) and the material input oriented, ecological data (Y-axis). The respective values represent company-specific information, since they correspond to relative values of the overall company. The assessment is accordingly based on only two indicators that represent process costs as well as lifecycle-wide environmental impact data.

The goal of an ecological-economic optimisation of the product range and the internal processes is to include (in the scope of the eco-efficient objective function) as many as possible product variants and production processes of the company portfolio. Both, optimised products and processes, contribute to an increased resource productivity of the entire enterprise while simultaneously contributing to cost reductions.

3.2.5 REA and Data Collection Levels

The REA tool can be implemented or introduced in enterprises on a site, process and product level. The individual levels and the respective data collection steps are elaborated in the following sections.

The level of application depends on the company, internal and operational circumstances. The exploitation of the possible potentials depends on the expense and effort associated with them. Influencing factors include, for example, the absolute resource consumption, the ratio of material costs to the total company costs and the availability of the data.

REA on Company Level

The objective of the REA is to achieve transparency regarding internal material flows. When introducing Resource Efficiency Accounting, it is suitable to analyse the three levels: site, process and product. In a first step, the enterprise is viewed as a black box, and all incoming and outgoing material and energy flows of the company are registered. These material and energy flows are not assessed at this point, since this step is chiefly concerned with creating an initial overview of the corporate input and outputs.

For the most part, ecological input data is already available in companies (e.g. in Purchasing) or can be derived with little effort from existing information systems. Furthermore, there is a usually number of employees within a company that can provide information on material consumption. For example, the warehouse management department usually has data on consumption quantities and pertinent departments. Department heads and shift managers generally know which machines have downtimes and standstills and how much scrap is produced.

Data on the economic dimension is mostly already available in enterprises within the scope of other information systems[23] and can be taken from the cost and performance accounting or the business accounting (also see Section 3.1.4). For the cost accounting related analysis of a company's material flows, the accuracy with which the cost centre structure reflects the real material and energy flows of the company is a crucial factor. The following table shows where certain data can most frequently be found within an enterprise.

---

[23] See Hallay/ Pfriem 1992, p. 57

Table 3.1. Potential information sources and pertinent input-output balance data

Information Source	Available Data/ Information
Purchasing, Inbound Warehouse	• Goods received as indicated on delivery notes • Possible catch weight of materials • Type and amount of packaging materials used for incoming packaging
Interim Storage, Outbound Warehouse, Internal Logistics	• Consumption quantities of raw, production and process materials and pre-products for the individual departments, sites, machines, processes (via material requisition cards) • Annual inventory data • Quantities, volumes and weights of the manufactured intermediate and end products • Type and amount of packaging materials used for outbound packaging
Department Head, Shift Manager, Machine Operator	• Consumption quantities of raw, production and process materials and intermediate products • Energy/ water consumption data • Cost information • Type and quantity of waste/ scrap, volume of waste water
Environmental Protection Officer/ Management	• Consumption quantities of raw, production and process materials • Energy/ water consumption data • Figures related to type and quantities of waste water/ waste/ scrap • Emissions data
Waste/ Scrap/ Hazardous Goods Manager	• Specific waste/ scrap quantities and types • Allocation of waste/scrap quantities and types • Charge materials and quantity of hazardous goods/ substances • Storage/ location/ disposal of hazardous goods and substances • Recycling/ separation/ treatment • Data on emission volumes and types

Table 3.1 (Cont.)

Bookkeeping, Accounting	• Prices and quantities of pre-products, raw, production and process materials by means of registered incoming invoices • Costs and amounts of energy/ water consumption and waste water disposal as derived from the monthly/ annual financial statements of the supplier(s)/ waste disposal company • Data concerning waste/ scrap quantities, disposal routes and incurred costs from the invoices issued by the waste disposal companies • Costs incurred for handling emissions (e.g. filters)
Cost Accounting Controlling, Finance Department	• Primary (direct) costs of cost centres (e.g. for the material consumption/ requirement of individual processes/ machines) • Overhead (indirect) costs of cost centres (most often production and process costs, administration, lighting, etc.) • Analysis of the cost trends over time • Analysis of the cost trends according to cost categories

The input-output analysis has proven to be a practical method for collecting such data.[24] It is a collection and information tool, in which all relevant material and energy flows related to a reference period are structured and collected in accordance with a specified, comparable methodology.

In an input-output analysis, the way in which the data is collected should enable allocation of the corresponding rucksack factors in the form of material intensities, e.g. in kilograms or tons. Moreover, internal balances should be designed in a way that permits them to be continuously maintained and updated.

At the conclusion of the input-output analysis, material flow data is provided at the company level; the data can be used for formulating long-term company objectives and assigning precise indicators for evaluating these objectives in an understandable manner. Thus, for example, a reduction in the internal material flows by a certain factor can be controlled by means of an annual input-output balance. In addition, it is possible to reconcile such material flow data with economic indicators in

---

[24] See Hallay/ Pfriem 1992, p. 58

order to determine the resource productivity of the entire enterprise. Within the scope of internal and external communication, the results can be made available to stakeholders, such as employees or customers.

REA on Process Level

On the process level, the data collected in the input-output analysis is assigned, on a usage basis, to the individual production processes. This serves the purpose of identifying which company processes are responsible for what material and energy consumption. A process is to be understood as a sequence of functionally, spatially and temporally interconnected job steps, which aims at achieving a specific end result via the use of materials and energies.[25]

The black box view of the enterprise is resolved by representing the individual process in a process diagram. The process diagram can thus be oriented on available material flow plans or similar information and has flow diagram properties. The diagram shows the processes with their reciprocal interdependencies. The connecting links between the processes are the internal material and energy flows as well as the information flows. Separate input-output balances are prepared for the identified processes, thus ensuring that the share of each process in relation to the company's total material and energy flow is made transparent. The procedure for the corporate process analysis is described in the following.

The processes interact with the environment via material flows that enter or leave the company. The processes are only functionally linked in the process diagram, i.e. the flow factors are not quantified yet.

---

[25] See Hallay/ Pfriem 1992, p. 80

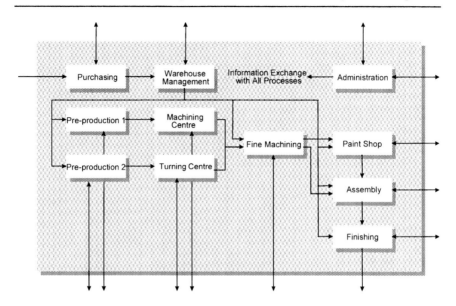

Fig. 3.1. Exemplary process diagram of a metal processing company

In a second step, the material flows are quantified within the scope of the process accounting. The process accounting aims at structuring and balancing the inputs and outputs of the individual processes to allow material intensities to be linked to the results in a further step. For the purpose of further structuring, it is suitable to subdivide the inputs into raw materials, process and production materials, energy and energy carriers. Wear and tear of operating resources is inherent in every production process, which is the reason why the operating resources have to be proportionally taken into account as material inputs when determining the total material consumption. In an initial approximation, it is possible to "quantitatively write off" the operating resources by means of linear depreciation over the period of their average useful life. Tool wear also falls into this category. Furthermore, other inputs also have to be included, such as material consumption arising from the services required for the process. A similar differentiation is carried out on the output side. The analysis of the output side is necessary for linking processes and procedures. Internal outputs are forwarded to downstream processes within the company. As a rule, the outputs comprise the main product of the process under consideration as well as internally processed by-products. External outputs consist of all the by-products (provided they are not internally processed), emissions, waste and residue materials, waste water, etc. of the process.

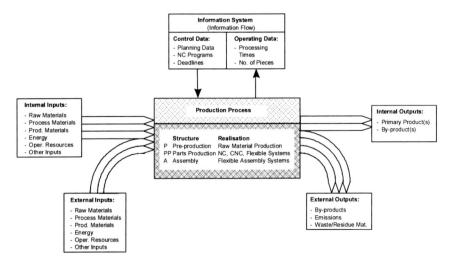

Fig. 3.2. Inputs and outputs of a production process

For each identified process, a separate input-output balance is created that includes all inputs and outputs in a structured form. The material flow factors are specified in standardised weight units such as kilograms (kg), in order to allocate to them, in the next step, the ecological rucksack in the form of material intensities.[26] To this end, an appropriate temporal or quantitative reference quantity is specified for assigning the material flow factors. This can be, e.g., a production shift or 1000 pieces of a defined intermediate product. The determination of the material intensity of a specific process is not based on the sum of all the inputs of a process: the (end) product to be manufactured is produced from raw and process materials on a step-by-step basis. Raw and process materials are counted at their point of entry into the production process. If they appear in further processing steps, they are not recorded again, otherwise the multiple counting would result in all of the company's inputs being cumulatively allocated to the last process (e.g. final inspection). It would then be impossible to perform a hot spot analysis on the process level focused on material or energy consumption. Consequently, *internal inputs* in the form of raw materials and process materials are not included in the equation on the process level. The basis for determining the material intensity of a process therefore results from the determined input quantities minus the internal raw and process materials. The determined materials and energy

---

[26] Two exceptions are electricity and water, which are specified in kWh and MJ, respectively.

consumptions are then correlated to the associated material intensities. The result of each of the individual inputs is described by means of the five MIPS categories, which are summed up in the next step for the purpose of determining the total material intensity of the process. The water and air categories are disregarded in the determination of the TMR value (see Section 3.2.3).

Since cost accounting does not usually allocate detailed individual costs for each input factor to individual processes, the costs of the processes are collected in a similar procedure.[27] This procedure is relatively simple, since the specific consumption quantities can be taken from the process-based input-output balances. The costs of the individual inputs for the entire company are available, but they only have to be allocated via consumption quantities and keys. Practical experience shows that the appropriate allocation and determination of process costs already results in a different picture of the company; often subprocesses which at times had been classified as rather irrelevant are now identified as significant cost drivers. The result of the process analysis is described by means of *a resource efficiency portfolio* on process level. It serves as basis of a "screening process" for identifying economic cost drivers and ecologically relevant areas within a company. The resource efficiency portfolio divides the processes with respect to the cost (EUR) and material/ energy consumption (based on material intensities) categories into four quadrants. The high and low rating is determined on a company-specific basis and is a relative index of all processes of a company.

---

[27] For more information refer to Schaltegger/ Müller 1998 or US Environmental Protection Agency 1998.

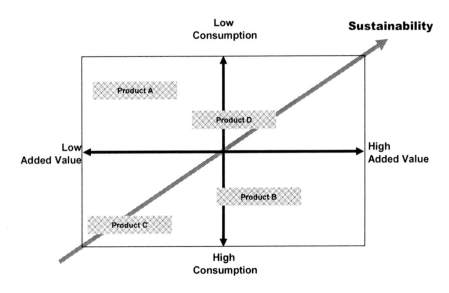

Fig 3.3. Example of a Resource Efficiency Portfolio on the process level

In the example (see Figure 3.3.), the paint shop would be the internal hot spot of the company. In regards to the goal of optimisation, processes should move into the premachining position of the chart. Various recommendations for action now arise as a result of allocating the individual processes to the respective quadrants (see Table 3.2).

Table 3.2. Action strategies for process optimisation derived from the resource efficiency portfolio on process level

	High Costs	Low Costs
Low Consumption	Selective approach, analysis and, if applicable, optimisation of individual cost factors	Good ecological performance and low economic relevance; thus no acute need for action
High Consumption	High ecological and economic relevance: top priority, hot spot on process level, systematic search for savings and substitution options	Selective approach, analysis and, if applicable, optimisation of individual input factors

The effective reduction of materials and energy is crucial to the economic-ecological success of the enterprise as a whole. The highest potentials result from the "high/ high" categories. They should be assigned top priority and could be the first processes to be subjected to an in-depth analysis, for example within the scope of an environmental protection program, since optimisation can result in the greatest savings effects here. Moreover, strategies for action can also be developed for the other quadrants; the respective processes then have to be handled in accordance with these strategies.

Depending on the objective of the internal process analysis, it can be of interest to disregard single factors when calculating the material intensity of a process. In some cases, for example materials that are used for a product (i.e. all raw materials) are determined by the design and should not be included in optimisation considerations within the course of a process analysis. In such cases, it can then be suitable to assess the process using only the material intensities of the deployed production materials and operating resources as well as the energy consumption.

REA on Product Level

Along with the process optimisations on product level, REA focuses on optimising the product range. To this end, REA strives to identify exemplary products in terms of eco-efficiency criteria. In this case optimisations potentials on the process level should have been realised. For a further optimisation on the product level, the company should have at least two different product ranges that provide a similar or identical customer benefit.

"Mass-based accounting" refers to a systematic classification and arrangement of the internal material and energy flows for each (end) product. The goal is to allocate the total consumption of the company to the manufactured products on a usage basis. Direct (individual) masses that are directly used for a product can be directly assigned to the product. Overhead (shared) masses cannot be directly allocated to a product, since they apply to several products at the same time (e.g. lighting or material inputs related to administration). In mass accounting, they have to be allocated to mass centres via an allocation key. In principle, mass centres comprise all of the operating equipment used for the production, distribution and sales of several products. Ideally, mass centres and cost centres are identical, thus facilitating the allocation process.

It becomes clear that in order to determine the internal material and energy flows of each (end) product, using a relatively detailed procedure, the consumption values of the individual processes can be summed up and allocated. The procedure is based on the results of the input-output analysis and the internal process analysis. The more detailed the preceding steps were carried out, the lower the effort required for the internal mass accounting. The material intensity values are included at the end of the calculation, when all inputs per product are summed up. The costs also form the basis for the assessment in the economic dimension. If a detailed cost accounting system exists, the values for calculatory individual unit costs can theoretically be adopted. Practical experience has demonstrated that a precise tracking and allocation of the costs determined on the basis of the material and energy flows can lead to a very different result.[28] Similar to the procedure for the ecological dimension, the individual cost factors of the processes have to be assigned to the products. As previously mentioned, an analysis of the existing keys for overhead costs (e.g. for energy consumption) is particularly important. It is precisely in that area where the largest number of deviations usually arises.

A one-sided cost accounting does not appear suitable here,[29] since in contrast to the process level, on which the manufacturing costs are especially relevant in regards to economic analysis,[30] relative factors in the form of added value have a larger economic significance at the product level. By means of profit per unit or contribution margins, the determined unit costs can therefore be used to generate information on the economic-efficiency of individual products.

Analogous to the analysis on the process level, the products are again arranged in a resource efficiency portfolio. In the following diagram (Figure 3.4.), the products are mapped according to their added value (EUR) and their material and energy consumption (based on material intensities). Again the border between high and low is determined on a company-specific basis. It is important to mention once again that this analysis deals with product alternatives. That means that product A can be substituted by product B, without significantly changing the benefit(s) for the customer/ consumer.

---

[28] For more information, please see e.g. Wagner/ Strobel 2003
[29] See Haake 1996, p. 21
[30] See Gotsche 1995, p. 10 et seq.

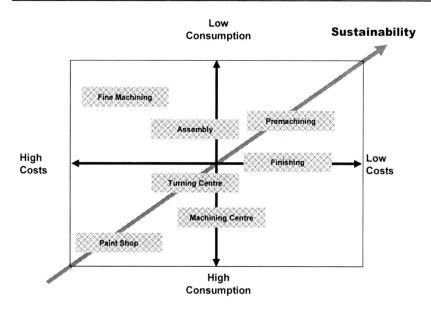

Fig. 3.4. The resource efficiency portfolio on the product level

Action strategies for product optimisation can be derived from the respective resource efficiency portfolios. The table 3.3 below provides an overview.

Table 3.3. Action strategies for product optimisation derived from the respective resource efficiency portfolio on product level

	Low Contribution Margin/ Profit per Unit	High Contribution Margin/ Profit per Unit
Low Consump-tion	Ecologically sound products; identifying potential(s) for increasing added value, e.g. using targeted marketing as low MI product	Economically and ecologically successful products; sales promotion through marketing as sustainable products
High Consump-tion	Less economically and ecologically advantageous products; aim should be substitution of products; if necessary tracing the causes on process level can be useful	Economically sound products; thus analysis of ecological weak spots via examination of substitution options for the used high-consumption or energy-intensive materials

For the discussion regarding the optimisation potentials, it was assumed that the products being analysed provide the same customer benefits and that process optimisation has already been implemented to the greatest possible extent. Therefore, the question to be addressed is: What suitable strategy should be defined if all optimisation potentials have been exhausted, but the economically successful products have a comparably high material and energy consumption? In this case, a more precise examination of the usage phase can be helpful. Potentials for reducing the consumption per defined service unit can especially be identified for use-intensive products. The difference between production and use intensive products is, that the production phase dominates the lifecycle-wide material consumption (e.g. furniture). With use intensive products the utilisation phase of the product is linked to the most dominant material consumption (e.g. washing machine). Thus, optimisation of the utilisation phase, e.g. by extending the product's service life, is in this case of central importance. In this regard, individual products are no longer assessed, but rather the services associated with the product. This approach attempts to emphasise a long-term service orientation and as a result, describe a two-fold effect: on one hand, the material intensity can be reduced, and on the other, additional benefits can be generated for the customer/ consumer.

Therefore a sustainable enterprise should aim at optimising the entire life cylce of a product. This plays a particularly important role in regards to product conception and design, since it is during these stages that the material consumption of the production, the utilisation phase and the recycling/ disposal phases are determined. A consideration of lifecycle aspects within the scope of the product design thus comprises optimisation of the material composition, reduction of the resource-consumption of the production and utilisation phases, a high repair and recycling capability of the end product as well as the disposal of residues and waste materials.[31] The economic dimension also calls for the early inclusion of these aspects during the production and product planning stages, since it is here that approx. 80% of the accrued costs are determined for the development, manufacturing and utilisation of products.[32]

REA Success Factors and Implementation Concept

As a central success factor for the implementation of the REA, the topic of resource efficiency should not be considered separately in management/ staff departments or specialised departments, but rather across all company

---

[31] See Schmidt-Bleek/ Tischner 1995, p. 21
[32] See Tischner 2001

departments and divisions. In the implementation projects, teams comprising five until eight people from various departments were formed within the companies. This approach was proved applicable, since the different experts could contribute their special know-how to the process. Furthermore, it created a basis for the company-wide acceptance of the REA.

The REA method presented here is based on detailed information about internal material and energy flows as well as the corresponding costs. Depending on the status of the cost accounting systems existing in the company, those costs sometimes have to be specially evaluated and allocated. As this process is a complex process, introduction of the REA on the basis of the described approach is dependent on the use of financial and personnel resources. However, this expense and effort is mainly required during the early stage of the project.

For the implementation a project team consisting of employees with key qualifications and competencies from all areas of the enterprise should be formed. To this end, the team should especially comprise employees who (1) possess experience and know-how regarding raw materials, consumption and purchasing quantities and who are in contact with suppliers and thus have an overview of the scope of delivery, delivery times, etc., (2) have a technical overview as well as longstanding employment with the company and therefore have precise knowledge on internal procedures, processes, operations, etc. and/ or (3) have IT experience or are in charge of operational/production control.

Based on the findings and experiences of the CARE project, a qualification concept was developed for conveying the contents, methodology and implementation of REA.[33] The concept consisted of four modular, interdependent qualification components to support employee training, the establishment of sufficient process transparency, the active inclusion and commitment on the part of the employees and the permanent embedding of the REA in the enterprise. Experience has proven that it is practical to design the introduction phase as a moderated process. The first step is therefore to designate someone in charge. This can be either a competent employee or an external moderator. His task is to plan and carry out the training measures and organise the activities. In principle, the REA is suitable for any company, regardless of size or sector. Nevertheless, company-specific differences exist, which can be either conducive or obstructive.[34] An in-depth implementation as described in the previous section may therefore be less feasible under real conditions. Material and

---

[33] See http://care-oekoeffizienz.de
[34] See Busch/ Beucker 2004, p. 142 et seq.

energy flow analysis can be associated with a high amount of expenses and effort. Especially for companies that are dealing with the topics of environmental costs and resource efficiency for the first time, it is often difficult to justify such expenses, since the cost-benefit ratio is hard to determine in advance. Furthermore, small and medium sized enterprises are frequently faced with an entirely different problem: they lack the necessary capacities required for an implementation process.

In this case they can conduct a more general initial analysis using a less complex model. The following section briefly outlines how a less complex "introductory" model – thus particularly appropriate for small and medium-sized enterprises – can be implemented on the process/company and product levels.

1. On process/ company level, the goal is to improve the eco-efficiency of the entire company by means of the targeted optimisation of a process. As a first step, the primary material and energy consumptions can be determined (as a guide number, 6-10 are sufficient). Usually, a complete input-output balance does not have to be prepared for this purpose. The relevant core factors are sufficient for a first analysis. The required annual consumption figures as well as the associated costs can e.g. be obtained from accounting. The corresponding total annual consumption figures are then linked with the respective material intensities[35], with the result being the lifecycle-wide impact of the most significant material and energy flows. This enables identification of the company's central consumption value(s). The next step is to identify the internal process that plays the main role in the consumption or processing and which, according to a subjective assessment, has or is presumed to have an optimisation potential. In general, these are processes, which also give rise to the greatest cost saving potentials. This process is thus also the internal hot spot; the eco-efficiency objective function strives to implement optimisation here, since this could lead to the most effective impact in terms of the entire company.
2. When focussing on product optimisation, the step of outlining and mapping the internal material and energy flows can be bypassed within the scope of an initial optimisation strategy. For the purposes of defining the eco-efficiency objective function, the main component(s) (guide number: 90% of the total weight) of products for which there are alternative production options should be identified first. The result should comprise specific weight information for each main component that is used for the end product. The respective product data can then be

---

[35] See http://www.mips-online.info

linked with the material intensities and subsequently summed up. The result describes the lifecycle-wide environmental impact of the various product alternatives. For the economic dimension, the relative profit share can be calculated. For this, the production costs of each product are taken from the cost and activity accounting. If there is insufficient information in regards to this, approximation values for the production costs can be determined using the accounting pertaining to the previously identified main component. The difference between the selling price and the production costs can then be formulated as the profit share of each product. The profit share in relation to the respective production costs can be designated as a relative profit share. In conjunction with the environmental impact, this value forms the basis for the eco-efficiency assessment of the product alternatives. The objective function can then either be a sales-increase of the product with the best economic-ecological performance or optimisation of the product with the worst result.

3.3 Case Study: Toshiba Europe

3.3.1 Initial Situation and Objective

Toshiba Europe GmbH - Regensburg Operations (TRO) is part of the globally operating Toshiba Group, which manufactures high-quality devices for the office, entertainment and medical electronics sectors. At the Regensburg/ Germany site, computer notebooks in a variety of models are produced and configured for the European market from assembly kits or from semi-finished products. Assembly and configuration processes take place in various production lines with varying levels of production depth ('Semi-Finished-Goods', 'Final Assembly and Test' and 'Frame'). Regensburg is a site with relatively low production depths. In principle, the consideration of lifecycle-wide environmental aspects is consequently of particular importance at the site, since this is the only way of providing effective decision-making support that maps the actual environmental impacts. Toshiba has undertaken to comply with internationally applicable environmental protection guidelines for the purpose of promoting environmental protection at all sites. A validated environmental management system in accordance with EMAS (EC eco-audit directive 1862/93) has already been in place at the Regensburg site since 1996. In line with the implementation of the environmental management system, the measurement and improvement of environmental performance are the key objectives of TRO's environmental management.

The aim of the CARE implementation project at TRO was to establish a systematic eco-controlling system at the Regensburg site. In this context, the existing environmental performance indicators (called "eco-efficients") should be more specifically assigned to specific causative agents. Furthermore, the environmental management system was to be expanded with a systematic and parallel consideration of the material flow related costs. In addition, the eco-controlling system should also be transferable to other Toshiba Group sites.

The Resource Efficiency Accounting method appeared suitable for generating pertinent indicators and integrating them into an ecological-economic decision-making system. The data collection and analysis steps could largely be supported by the already existing IT systems.

3.3.1 Procedure

With the aid of the EMIS Umberto®, an internal material flow analysis was performed in the course of the project. The results concluded that a large portion of the required materials and energy were already being efficiently used. Nevertheless the material flow analysis made evident that in addition to the product related primary mass flows, the mass flows attributed to the supplier packaging in the 'Final Assembly and Test' production line is conspicuously large. At the Regensburg site, supplier packaging particularly amasses due to the delivery of key components used for notebook production. The cost effects and environmental impact associated with the packaging were therefore subjected to a detailed analysis. As measurement indicators for analysing the resource efficiency of different transport packagings, the waste material costs and material intensity (MI) values of different packaging variants were recorded and compared. Figure 3.5 provides an example of the material flow analysis for individual relevant to packaging.

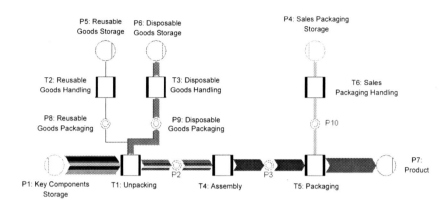

Fig. 3.5. Detailed analysis of packagings, utilising Umberto®

The detailed analysis found that transport packaging used by the various suppliers can greatly differ in terms of cost effects and environmental impacts at the site. The identified cost effects and environmental impacts of the packaging variants were compared with one another and contrasted as best case and worst case scenarios.

In detail, the waste material costs recorded for each packaging variant comprise the following:

- Unpacking costs: costs attributed to unpacking components at the site.
- Repacking costs: costs attributed to repacking components into boxes for supplying the production lines.
- Handling costs: costs attributed to transporting the packaging waste to the company's own disposal facility as well as to the sorting involved.
- Disposal costs: costs attributed to the waste being removed by various disposal companies.

In addition to the cost blocks described above, transport-specific costs for the different packaging variants were identified in relation to the country of origin, volume and weight.

The environmental impact of the packaging variants was determined in the form of streamlined LCAs[36] and with the inclusion of the corresponding MIT values as impact indicators for the respective lifecycle phases (production, utilisation and recycling/ disposal).

---

[36] For more on the Streamlined LCA approach, see Christiansen et al. 1997

3.3.3 Results of the Resource Efficiency Accounting at Toshiba

The most significant results of the analysis can be summarised as follows:

Costs: from among the cost blocks described above, the transport as well as the unpacking and repacking costs represent the largest cost effects of the supplier packaging. The potential savings justify the integration of the results into the existing procedures for evaluating suppliers. In comparison to the unpacking/ repacking costs, the handling and disposal costs reflect a relatively small share. They amount to less than 1% of the total sum of the waste material costs and transport costs. *Environmental Impacts:* the largest share of the environmental impacts attributed to supplier packaging arises from transporting the packaged products via air freight. In contrast, the environmental impact of the packaging itself amounts to only a small share (< 10%) of the environmental impacts caused by packaging.

In regards to the selection and optimisation of supplier packaging, the following statements can be derived from the aforementioned results:

• Reducing the quantity, mass and volume of packaging takes top priority from both a cost and environmental protection standpoint. Large mass and large volumes of packaging have a high correlation to high transport and personnel costs.
• The efficient utilisation, planning and arrangement of air transport represent a high priority from both a cost and environmental protection perspective. Since virtually all components are delivered via air freight, stopovers should be eliminated and the packaging volume should be as small and light-weight as possible.

The pivotal result of the Resource Efficiency Accounting at TRO thus underscored the fact that the various used materials do not represent the decisive factor for the optimisations, but rather how such materials are utilised and deployed. In this context, it was essential to not only precisely analyse the procedures and processes, but especially examine the lifecycle-wide environmental impacts through the use of an integrated method.

3.3.4 IT Based and Organisational Implementation of Resource Efficiency Accounting at Toshiba

In order to permanently embed Resource Efficiency Accounting as a tool for assessing supplier packaging at Toshiba, the results will most likely be integrated into the production database and incorporated into future business processes. In terms of IT support for analysing supplier packageing, excellent prerequisites exist at Toshiba, as component and product relevant data is already stored for quality assurance purposes. Since defined packaging variants can be assigned to specific components, expanding the master data structures in Toshiba's information system can enable allocation of environmental and cost-specific packaging indicators as well as an analysis of the actual arising costs and environmental impacts. The input and maintenance of the costs and environmental impacts in the form of MI values, as is required for such an analysis, is facilitated by a tool managed by the environmental management team at the Regensburg site. A prototype of the assessment tool was integrated into TRO's business information system during the course of the project.

The packaging-specific indicators can be evaluated using resource efficiency portfolios. The different departments at the Regensburg site are thus provided with specific evaluations for ecological-economic optimisations. The results of the analysis are mapped in the resource efficiency portfolio as economic values (euro per piece) and ecological values (material intensity per piece). This enables the direct comparison of materials, processes or products in regards to the ecological and economic characteristics. Two typical packaging alternatives of various suppliers are compared in figure 3.6, with the packaging from Supplier A being the more cost-effective and environmentally friendlier option.

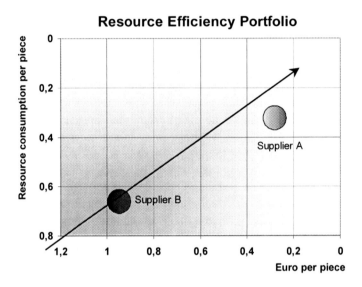

Fig. 3.6. Comparison of suppliers by means of supplier packaging in the resource efficiency portfolio

By defining specific controlling processes, the analysis can be integrated into existing TRO processes, for example supplier rating or quality management. Moreover, the results can be incorporated into existing assessment systems, e.g. management reviews. At present, the transferability of the method to further production lines is being tested.

References

Bartelmus P, Bringezu S, Moll S (2001) Dematerialization, Environmental Accounting and Resource Management. WIKUE, Wuppertal (URL: http://europa.eu.int/comm/environment/enveco/studies2.htm#26)

Busch T, Beucker S, (2004) Computergestützte Ressourceneffizienz-Rechnung in der mittelständischen Wirtschaft. Schlussbericht. Untersuchungsschritte und – ergebnisse aus dem Kernprojekt und den Umsetzungsprojekten des Forschungsprojekts care. Wuppertal Stuttgart (URL: http://www.tib.uni-hannover.de)

Busch T, Orbach T (2003) Umweltkostenrechnung – Arten von Umweltkosten, praktische Verfahren und Entwicklungsperspektiven. In: Lutz U, Nehls-Sahabandu M (eds.) Betriebliches Umweltmanagement: Grundlagen, Methoden, Praxisbeispiele. Gonimos Publishing, Neidlingen, Sektion 01/03

Bundesumweltministerium, Umweltbundesamt (eds) (2001) Handbuch Umweltcontrolling, 2th edn, Munich

Christiansen et al. (1997) Simplifying LCA: Just a Cut? SETAC EUROPE, Brussels (Final Report from the SETAC-EUROPE LCA-Screening and Streamlining Working Group)

Dyllick T, Hockerts K (2002) Beyond the Business Case for Corporate Sustainability. In: Business Strategy and the Environment 11/2002, pp 130-141

European Environment Agency (ed) (2003) Europe's environment: the third assessment, Environmental assessment report no 10, Copenhagen (URL: http://reports.eea.eu.int/environmental_ assessment_report_2003_10/en)

Faßbender-Wynands, E (2001) Umweltorientierte Lebenszyklusrechnung – Instrument zur Unterstützung des Umweltkostenmanagements, Cologne

Fischer H, Blasius R (1995) Umweltkostenrechnung. In: Bundesumweltministerium/ Umweltbundesamt (ed) (1995) Handbuch Umweltcontrolling, 1th edn, Munich

Fischer H, Lichtblau K, Meyer B, Scheelhaase J (2004) Wachstums- und Beschäftigungsimpulse rentabler Materialeinsparungen. In: Wirtschaftsdienst – Zeitschrift für Wirtschaftspolitik, no 84, pp 247-254

Gotsche B (1995) Wertschöpfungsanalyse der deutschen Stahlindustrie. Wuppertal Papers, no 36, Wuppertal

Hallay H, Pfriem R, (1992) Öko-Controlling – Umweltschutz in mittelständischen Unternehmen. Campus, Frankfurt

Haake J (1996) Langlebige Produkte für eine zukunftsfähige Entwicklung – eine ökonomische Analyse. Wuppertal Papers, no 62, Wuppertal

Heupel T, Wendisch N (2002) Prozessbasierte Umweltkostenrechnung – Implementation in KMU in Deutschland, Polen und Tschechien. IÖB-Arbeitspapier Nr. 2, University of Siegen

Hockerts K, Hamschmidt J, Dyllick T (1999) Prozesskostenoptimierung durch integriertes Ressourcenmanagement – Einbindung von Umweltmanagementsoftware in die betriebliche Kostenrechnung am Beispiel SAP R/3. IWÖ-Diskussionsbeitrag Nr. 74, St. Gallen

Jasch C (2001) Was sind Umweltkosten? In: Ökologisches Wirtschaften 06/01, pp 18-19

Landesanstalt für Umweltschutz Baden-Württemberg (ed) (2000) Prozessorientierte integrierte Managementsysteme. 1th edn, Karlsruhe

Letmathe P, Wagner G.R. (2002) Umweltkostenrechnung. In: Küpper H-U, Wagenhofer A (eds) (2002) Handwörterbuch Unternehmensrechnung und Controlling, 4th edn, Stuttgart, pp 1988-1997

Loew T (2001) Kein „one best way" im Umweltkostenmanagement. In: Ökologisches Wirtschaften 06/01, pp 10-11

Remer D (1997) Einführen der Prozesskostenrechnung – Grundlagen, Methodik, Einführung und Anwendung der verursachungsgerechten Gemeinkostenzurechnung. Schäfer-Poeschel, Stuttgart

Ritthoff M, Rohn H, Liedtke C (2003) MIPS berechnen – Ressourcenproduktivität von Produkten und Dienstleistungen. Wuppertal Spezial 27, Wuppertal

Schaltegger S, Müller K (1998) Calculating the True Profitability of Pollution Prevention. In: Bennett M, James P (eds.) (1998) The Green Bottom Line, Sheffield, Greenleaf Publishing, pp 86-99

Schaltegger S, Sturm A (1990) Ökologische Rationalität. In: Die Unternehmung, no 4, pp 117-131

Schmidt-Bleek F (2004) Der ökologische Rucksack – Wirtschaft für eine Zukunft mit Zukunft. Stuttgart Leipzig

Schmidt-Bleek F (1994) Wieviel Umwelt braucht der Mensch? MIPS – das Maß für ökologisches Wirtschaften. Berlin Basel Boston

Schmidt-Bleek F, Tischner U (1995) Produktentwicklung: Nutzen gestalten – Natur schonen. WIFI, Vienna

Schulz W-F, Kreeb M, Letmathe P (2000) Betriebliches Umweltkostenmanagement – Mit externen Umweltkosten rechnen? Dknw/ Universität Hohenheim/ Ruhr Universität Bochum, Berlin Bochum Witten-Herdecke

Seuring S (2001) Supply Chain Costing – Kostenmanagement in der Wertschöpfungskette mit Target Costing und Prozesskostenrechnung. Munich

Strobel M, Redmann C (2002): Flow Cost Accounting – An Accounting Approach based on the Actual Flows of Materials. In: Bennett M, Bouma J, Wolters T (eds) (2002) Eco-Efficiency in Industry and Science, Environmental Management Accounting – Informational and Institutional Developments, 9th edn, Doordrecht, Kluwer Academic Publishers, pp 67-82

Strobel M, Wagner B (1997) Strukturierung und Entwicklung der betrieblichen Stoff- und Energieflüsse. In: Fischer H, Wucherer C, Wagner B, Burschel C (eds) (1997) Umweltkostenmanagement – Kosten senken durch praxiserprobtes Umweltcontrolling. Carl Hanser Verlag, Munich Vienna, pp 28-57

Tischner U (2001) EcoDesign. In: Lutz U, Nehls-Sahabandu (eds.) (2003) Betriebliches Umweltmanagement – Grundlagen, Methoden, Praxisbeispiele. Gonimos Publishing

US Environmental Protection Agency (1998) An Introduction to Environmental Accounting as a Business Management Tool. In: Bennett M, James P (eds) (1998) The Green Bottom Line. Sheffield, Greenleaf Publishing, pp 61-85

Wagner B, Strobel M (2003) Flussmanagement für Produktionsunternehmen – Material- und Informationsflüsse nachhaltig gestalten. imu Augsburg/ Zentrum für Weiterbildung und Wissenstransfer Augsburg

Weizsäcker E-U von, Liedtke C, Seiler-Hausmann J-D (2004) Eco-efficiency and Beyond, Toward the Sustainable Enterprise. Greenleaf Publishing, Sheffield

Wiehle U, Diegelmann M, Deter H, Schömig P-N, Rolf M (2003) Kennzahlen für Investor Relations. cometics, Wiesbaden

Wuppertal Institut (ed) (2003) Tabelle mit Werten für die Materialintensität von Materialien und Energieträgern. (URL: http://www.mips-online.info)

4 Measuring Environmental Performance with EPM-KOMPAS Software Tool – Material Flow Analyses, Environmental Assessment and Success Control

Edeltraud Günther, Susann Kaulich

Edeltraud Günther, Department of Business Management and Economics, University of Technology Dresden, Germany
E-Mail: bu@mailbox.tu-dresden.de

Susann Kaulich, Department of Business Management and Economics, University of Technology Dresden, Germany
E-Mail: susann.kaulich@mailbox.tu-dresden.de

4.1 Decision Support: The Basic Principle

Within the scope of the demands and dynamics posed by the practice of measuring the performance and success of environmental management, the EPM-KOMPAS[1] is intended to be used and integrated within the internal decision making processes. The EPM-KOMPAS, a tool for controlling environmental performance measurement developed for small and medium-sized enterprises (SMEs), that offers not only reporting, but also decision functions, was developed for companies with the principle of decision support, the objective being to support these companies in integrating their environmental performance into the internal decision-making process.

In order to implement this basic decision support principle, the EPM-KOMPAS employs the principles of materiality (by identifying master parameters and performance drivers that the company can influence) and

---

[1] Developed within the scope of the research project EPM-KOMPAS financed by the German Federal Ministry of Education and Research: http://www.tu-dresden.de/wwbwlbu/forschung/laufende_projekte/epm_kompas/en/

individuality (by specifying individual action fields). This paper intends to answer the following questions:

- What are willingness and capability to perform?
- What should be measured?
- How does the EPM-KOMPAS tool work?
- How is the tool deployed in a case study?
- What strategic options does the EPM-KOMPAS offer?

4.2 Willingness and Capability to Perform: Commitment, Competence and Choice

The willingness to perform ("commitment") and the capability to perform ("competence") of a company are basic prerequisites for using the EPM-KOMPAS. At a strategic level, the individual willingness to improve environmental performance – in conjunction with the corresponding environmentally-oriented strategy and the introduction of an environmental management system – is assumed as a basis, since the starting point of every commitment made by a company is the commitment on the part of the executive management (environmental protection is a top level, high-priority issue) to allow environmental aspects to actually have an impact on entrepreneurial, business and management decisions. This degree of assumed responsibility – the willingness to environmental performance – is augmented by the capability to environmental performance as a strategic company objective. Analogous to the understanding of business and economic success potentials, this objective includes the maintenance and development of environmental performance potentials (Günther and Kaulich, 2003).[2] Ideally, this strategic objective is implemented with an environmentally-oriented strategy and by deploying an environmental management system. The idea of linking willingness and capability to perform can be taken from economic and social policies, in which the principle of linking individual willingness (of the economic subjects) with economic capability to perform (of society) is a key value. In this context, solidarity is rooted as a basic value, that will only be consistently practised by the members of a mutually supportive society if this solidarity is not overused or overstrained by others who conduct themselves in a less 'self-responsible' manner than could be expected from them. (Lampert and

---

[2] The SWOT (strengths, weaknesses, opportunities, threats) analysis method is applied by conducting an environment-related company internal and external analysis.

Althammer, 2001) The same applies to environmental performance. When willingness ("commitment") and capability to environmental performance ("competence") are combined with a positively developed normative level ("choice"), it leads to the formation of an interwoven 'triad of success at the socio-environmental success level (Steinle and Reiter, 2002). This success level is located at the transition point from the strategic to the operational level, as that is a crucial problem area for the practical implementation of strategically aligned tasks. For this reason, this link requires special regard, since in the end, the strategy is brought to life by employees on the operational level.

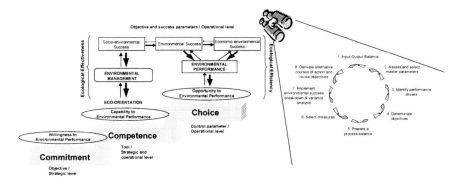

Fig. 4.1. Strategic and operational environmental performance and the EPM-KOMPAS at the operational level (Source: Günther and Kaulich, 2003)

Prerequisite No. 1: Willingness, capability and opportunities to environmental performance: commitment, competence and choice

4.3 Environmental Performance and Environmental Success: What Should Be Measured?

Since the EPM-KOMPAS is used within the scope of the demands and dynamics posed by the practice of measuring the performance and success of environmental management, a clarification as a further prerequisite has to be made in regards to what this means in internal practice. This is necessitated by the fact that the definition and term of performance is subject to a wide variety of interpretations in the various scientific fields (e.g. physics, psychology, business administration), which in practice results in multiple uses (Gleich, 2001). Moreover, the question should be addressed as to whether defining environmental performance in accordance with EMAS II or ISO 14031 actually explains what it is that constitutes environmental performance. Based on this insight, various approaches to the term 'environmental performance' were compiled and analysed in order to establish a definition (see Figure 4.2.).

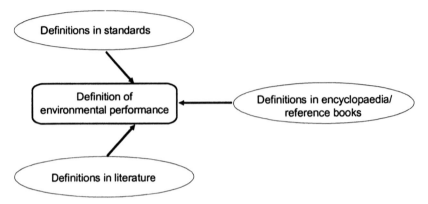

Fig. 4.2. Possible approaches to a working definition of environmental performance

An overview of the numerous existing performance definitions demonstrates that performance is basically conceived either as an activity in itself or as the result of an activity (Gleich, 2001). This basic concept is also widespread in business administration and economics and should therefore be transferred by analogical inference to the conceptual model of environmental performance. This results in two dimensions of environmental performance:

- the performance of the environmental management system (performance in the sense of activity), and
- performance in the sense of changes to internal environmental aspects and/ or environmental impacts (performance in the sense of the results of activity).

An impulse survey[3] conducted in 2002 found that approx. one-third of the persons questioned indicated environmental performance as defined by

---

[3] The short questionnaire was handed out in the INA Network panel of experts (www.ina-netzwerk.de) at the INA status seminar on 4 July 2002, in the forums, plenum and work groups; it was also sent to all network members via the INA Network's e-mail distributor. The study is not intended to be of a representative character; but does, however, serve the purpose of reflecting the various conceptual facets of environmental performance in regards to the performance measurement and sustainability existing in such a panel of experts in both research and practice and integrating the results into research work.

the existing standards while another third defined environmental performance as a decrease in environmental pollution, i.e. a *reduction of environmental aspects* in regards to the company/ a product/ a process. In contrast,
28.1 % of the answers indicated environmental performance as *the total of
environmental aspects* attributed to a company/ a product/ a process within
a certain period (see Figure 4.3.).[4] With 54.5 % of all answers, the
understanding of environmental performance conforming with the existing
standards explicitly refers to the specific ISO 14031 standard or the EMAS
II EU directive, with the majority of the respondents (83.3 %) clearly
mentioning the ISO 14031 standard (16.7 % for EMAS II). The remaining
45.5 % of the respondents described the content of the definition in their
own words, thus it was not possible to definitely determine which
standard/ directive forms the basis of the definition (see Figure 4.3).[5]

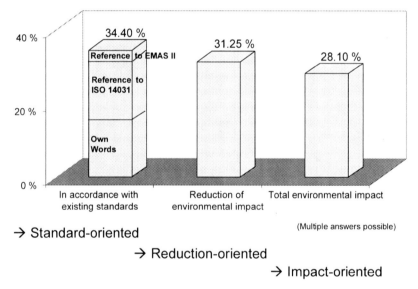

Fig. 4.3. Definitions of environmental performance[6]

With the two concrete conceptual directions arising from the impulse
survey (total environmental aspects and reduction of environmental
aspects) as further research objects, it becomes possible to create and use

---

[4] Percentages only refer to those respondents who indicated a conceptual model in
  question 2.
[5] Percentages only refer to those respondents who indicated a conceptual model in
  accordance with existing standards in question 2.
[6] Percentages only refer to those respondents who indicated a conceptual model in
  question 2.

the following matrix (see Table 4.1) in order to examine definition approaches by using the existing topic-specific literature:

Table 4.1. Matrix of environmental performance definitions

Environmental performance definition	Activity	Result of activity	Total environmental impact	Reduction of environmental impact
BMU (German Federal Ministry for the Environment) and FEA (German Federal Environmental Agency), 1997: Environmental Impact of Companies	☒	☑ [a]	☑	☒
Stahlmann and Clausen, 2000: "Environmental relief or revitalisation of natural environment directly or indirectly attributable to companies"	☑ [b]	☑ [c]	☒	☑ [d]
Wagner, 2003: "Aggregate index of emissions and inputs [...] or as an environmental rating"	☒	☑	☑	☒
Lankoski, 2000: "Environmental performance refers to the level of harmful environmental impacts [...] so that the smaller the harmful environmental impact the better the environmental performance and vice versa."	☒	☑	☒	☑
Kottmann et al., 1999: Environmental Impact (environmental performance as euphemistic variable)	☒	☑	☑ [e]	☑
Schaltegger et al., 2001: "Environmental performance is the total of a firm's behaviour towards the natural environment (i.e. its level of total resource consumption and emissions)."	☒	☑	☑	☒
ISO, 1999: "the results of an organization's management of its environmental aspects."	☑ [f]	☑ [g]	☑ [h]	☒ [i]
☒ Not applicable	☑ Applicable			

[a] These are recorded via indicators.
[b] Reference to revitalisation.
[c] Directly or indirectly caused environmental relief.

ᵈ This definition explicitly relates to the fact that environmental performance is only assumed if the changes to the environmental aspects were positive.
ᵉ In this context, environmental impact is understood as total environmental impact.
ᶠ Recording and mapping via management performance indicators.
ᵍ Recording and mapping via operational performance indicators.
ʰ Mapping via operational performance indicators.
ⁱ Represents the implicit goal, however, the definition does not explicitly focus on this aspect.

The analysis concludes that there are definitions that contain both conceptual models of the impulse survey. In addition, it was possible to ascertain definitions that only refer to one of the two models. Moreover, it can be noted that environmental performance is defined both as an activity and the result of an activity. It becomes evident that this does not lead to clarification in regards to the term of environmental performance, since depending on the literature used for determining a definition applicable to a company, the understanding varies significantly. In the course of ency-clopaedic research, it could be determined that a combination of the two word components "environment" and "performance" provides a practical starting point for developing a definition.

• In general, *environment* is understood as "the complex of physical, chemical, and biotic factors that act upon an organism or an ecological community and ultimately determine its form and survival". (Ency-clopaedia Britannica, 2004)
• *Business performance* in terms of manufacturing is defined as "fabrication or assembly of components into finished products on a fairly large scale". (Encyclopaedia Britannica, 2004)

Derived from that, environmental performance comprises the appli-cation (activity) or the result of the biotic or abiotic factors (environmental aspects) created in a company's production processes during a certain period of time, which directly or indirectly affect an organism, ecological community or symbiosis, as well as the effects arising from their inter-action. This definition conforms to the 'total environmental impact' category of the impulse survey.

Thus, *environmental performance* can be viewed as the *absolute result* of a company in regards to its environment. If the activities of a company do not directly relate to the environmental aspects of the company itself or if the impact of certain activities on the environmental aspects of a company cannot be directly measured, the environmental performance can also be recorded and assessed in the form of designating and describing these activities.[7] Therefore, both the absolute results of the environmental management activities are taken into consideration as well as those activities that do not result in directly measurable results in the environmental aspects of a company.

Thus, environmental performance is not a value descriptive of changes, but the absolute (annual) value which then serves as a basis for determining the environmental success (change index).

Environmental success is understood as the *intended difference between absolute environmental performance values* (in regards to the concrete environmental aspects of a company), i.e. as the difference between the current environmental performance value and an objective, since success is generally understood as a difference analysis. In line with the understanding of success as perceived in the business administration/ economics field, environmental success can assume both positive and negative values.

An explanation of these positive or negative values is rendered with the environmental success breakdown (see chapter 4.4.7) by breaking down the environmental success in regards to specified parameters in order to map the original environmental success achieved by a company.

> *Prerequisite No. 2*: Defining and recognising environmental performance and environmental success

4.4 The EPM-KOMPAS: How Does the Tool Work?

Specifying the system boundary is another prerequisite for the EPM-KOMPAS. In small and medium-sized enterprises (SMEs), a system boundary at company level (gate-to-gate) can be assumed. This delimitation corresponds to the one also selected for economic calculations. For each of the other selectable system boundaries (e.g. for products, processes, etc.), the tool can be individually applied according to the requirements of the company.

> *Prerequisite No. 3*: Specifying the system boundary

---

[7] Examples of this include employee training in environmental issues, rainforest reafforestation by companies that have no relation to forestry or the use of forests within the scope of their business activities.

In the following, the principle of the EPM-KOMPAS is explained by way of the individual EPM-KOMPAS steps (see Figure 4.4.).

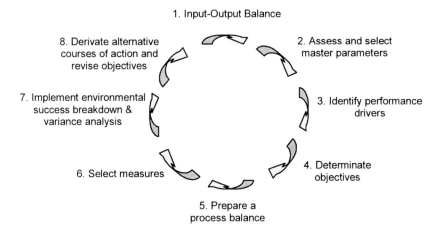

Fig. 4.4. The EPM-KOMPAS tool (Günther and Kaulich, 2003)

4.4.1 Step 1: Input/ Output Balance

In *Step 1* of the EPM-KOMPAS, the material and energy flows of a company are recorded in order to create the required data basis for the identification of significant environmental aspects. This context raises the question concerning a completeness requirement (recording of all environmental aspects of a company) versus a materiality standard (recording of all environmental aspects deemed substantial).

A recording of all material and energy flows of a company has to be viewed as unrealistic for small and medium-sized enterprises (SMEs), even with a company level system boundary. In this context, both project experiences and studies (Stefan et al., 1995) can be referenced, since it is particularly in the data collection sector that SMEs demonstrate deficits. With companies, the required necessary information concerning environment-relevant processes/ activities are more likely to be documented the bigger a company is. (Stefan et al., 1995)

Therefore, the EPM-KOMPAS meets the practicability requirements of SMEs and that is why the EPM-KOMPAS works with environmentally significant data comprising raw materials, auxiliary materials, hazardous materials, corporate energy values, waste and emissions (Steinle and Reiter, 2002). Here, the motto is: *Not complete, but feasible!* These priority 1 data are the minimum requirements to be met by the EPM-KOMPAS users and serve the purpose of making the tool manageable, especially for SMEs, and reducing complexity. Of course, any additional (already existing) data of the company can be integrated, but is not absolutely necessary for working with the tool.

4.4.2 Step 2: Environmental Assessment and Selection of Master Parameters

Step 2 covers the important assessment of this data basis in order to identify the corporate master parameters (significant environmental aspects). Thus, Step 2 implements the idea of qualified reduction the complexity in regards to the abundance of corporate environmental aspects, resulting in a few, significant criteria to be taken into account in a decision context – in practice, the term *master parameters* is used.

The basic concept of identifying the significant environmental aspects of a company is already integrated in EMAS II. The regulation encourages companies to determine which aspects have a significant environmental impact. (European Parliament and the Council of the European Union, 2001) To this end, EMAS II stipulates using criteria that is comprehensive, capable of independent checking, reproducible and made publicly available. In regards to the selection of an assessment method that can be used by SMEs, EMAS II is limited to statements regarding content and structure.

However, it is exactly this important step of assessing the collected data and, in order to reduce complexity, selecting significant environmental aspects (master parameters) for which SMEs need to be offered a simple and functioning assessment method that takes into account the data available in SMEs.

4.4.3 In Detail: Environmental Assessment Method for Master Parameter Determination

In order to enable companies, in particular SMEs, to assess the environmental aspects attributable to them and in turn take measures with respect to significant aspects, existing environmental aspects have to be assessed according to their environmental relevance. To facilitate this, a catalogue is created in the EPM-KOMPAS that contains the assessed environmental aspects along with their environmental assessment. In this context, the environmental aspects are assessed from two perspectives:

- Requirements of the society (qualitative assessment),[8] and
- State of the art in science (quantitative assessment).

Moreover, companies are enabled to store master parameters in the EPM-KOMPAS tool by a free choice mode.

Free Choice

The free choice of master parameters in the EPM-KOMPAS is possible if these parameters are already known by the company. This can be a result of third-party specifications and requirements (parent company, etc.) or the use of another, already existing assessment method, which can be not only of an environmental type, but also of an economic or social one.

Workshop with Impulse Questions in the Sense of a Multi-Stakeholder Dialogue

Of all the environmental assessment methods developed and used in practice up to now, only the ABC-classification method can be classified as a relatively widely used qualitative assessment method.

In order to open up the potentialities inherent to the stakeholder dialogue (Freeman, 1984) to SMEs and enable them to implement the perceived requirements put forth to them,[9] an active component along the lines of the ABC-classification method was integrated into the EPM-KOMPAS tool: a workshop based on the stakeholder approach with a silent moderator.

The Special Characteristic of the "Silent Moderator"

Impulse questions were stored for individual stakeholders maintained in the tool (these include competitors, customers, suppliers, management, employees, banks/ insurance companies/ shareholders, residents/ the interested public, legal requirements). Via systematic response, companies can gain an impression of their stakeholders' interests and the resultant master

---

[8] On the one hand, the reasons for considering societal aspects are rooted in a lack of knowledge concerning the cause and effect relationships of numerous environmental aspects and effects (i.e., the company needs other benchmarks for the assessment of environmental aspects), on the other hand, in the necessity for companies to include in their decisions the relevant stakeholder groups and their threat potential (e.g. boycotts, poor image, etc.).

[9] Perception means that a company can be subjectively affected, i.e., to what extent are external demands (coming from customers, suppliers, creditors, etc.) and internal demands (coming from management, employees, etc.) concerning the environmental aspects of a company noticed and taken into consideration.

parameters. It is possible to continue rating the obtained impulses as high, medium or low in regards to their relevance for the company. Thus, impulses are assessed according to their relevance and the master parameter derivation process is facilitated and assisted. The establishment of a company-internal task force for the joint processing of the impulse questions asked by the tool is an organisational implementation option for this procedure. In this context, the software assumes the role of a "silent moderator".

Automatic Calculation Based on the KOMPAS-Assessment by Günther/ Kaulich

As set out above, the free choice with which the EPM-KOMPAS is even opened regarding the results of every other environmental assessment method and the workshop as qualitative approach to implement the requirements of the society are two possibilities for the environmental assessment in the EPM-KOMPAS tool.

Apart from these possibilities a quantitative assessment method that results in automatically calculated parameters should also be implemented. This quantitative assessment in the EPM-KOMPAS is based on the concept of the impact categories[10]. With this concept, an approach was intentionally selected which comprises a transparent and multi-dimensional result that is not subject to aggregation, because at least the company itself has to decide on which its management of environmental performance to focus. Therefore, the assessment method should provide the company in particular with a multidimensional basis on which an effective decision could be taken.

Based on the impact categories in accordance to ISO 14042, which also form the orientation for the approach by the German Federal Environmental Agency, and for practicability considerations, the EPM-KOMPAS divides its impact categories into two groups: *company-internal impact categories and superordinate impact categories*. Human toxicity, eco-toxicity as well as hazard of fire and explosion and waste, which are also highly relevant to SMEs in terms of quality and risk aspects, were incorporated into the company-internal impact categories of the EPM-KOMPAS assessment method. Consideration of the energy consumption is recommended as an absolute, unweighted value.

---

[10] Which has already been integrated into the existing ISO 14042 standard (ISO, 2000).

In addition, the greenhouse effect, acidification, photo-oxidant formation and depletion of energy and material resources are considered to be *superordinate impact categories* (Federal Environmental Agency, 1999 and 2002).

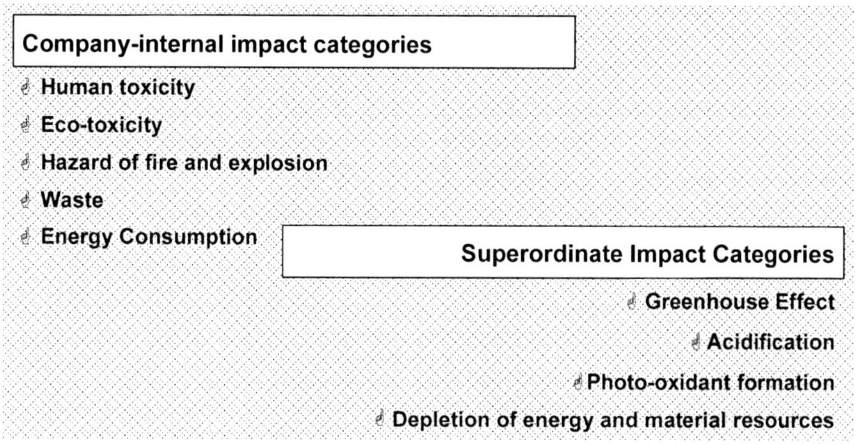

Fig. 4.5. Scope of company-internal and superordinate impact categories in the EPM-KOMPAS

In order to assess these company-internal and superordinate impact categories to be considered in a manner that is feasible for SMEs, recourse was taken to existing, science-based assessment methods, including, among others, the "Column Model" in accordance with TRGS 440,[11] emission factors, cumulated energy requirement (CER) and cumulated material requirement (CMR). The assessment of the company-internal impact categories of human toxicity, eco-toxicity as well as hazard of fire and explosion is based on the hazardous materials assessment according to the column model. By classifying hazardous substances according to their R-phrases and water hazard classes, the column model offers a ranking consisting of very high, high, medium, low and negligible hazard in regards to the three company-internal impact categories mentioned above. Apart from this environmental prioritisation, which functions independently of utilised quantities/ volumes, the quantities/ volumes and costs of the hazardous materials are included in the assessment method of the EPM-KOMPAS tool. In the waste category, the assessment is based on the

---

[11] See http://www.hvbg.de/e/bia/pra/spalte/spaltmod.pdf

classification according to the European Waste Catalogue and includes a comparison of quantities/ volumes and costs with the environmental ranking, as well. The additional consideration of the absolute amount of energy consumption is recommended. In order to sensitise companies to their specific share in contributing to the greenhouse effect, the corporate energy consumption is converted into CO_2 equivalents by using emission factors. The same approach is used to convert the corporate energy consumption into equivalents for the superordinate impact categories acidification and photo-oxidant formation. In addition to considering the raw materials and consumables that enter into the material balance as input and the resulting environmental impact attributed to the extraction and refining of raw materials, the superordinate impact category of depletion of energy and material resources also includes energy as a resource (Federal Environmental Agency, 1999). As proposed by the Federal Environmental Agency, the energy requirement for the extraction of raw materials and the production of consumables is incorporated as CER - cumulated energy requirement (Federal Environmental Agency, 2002). The CMR – cumulated material requirement – is used for the resources required for the extraction of raw materials and the production of consumables.[12]

The following *environmental performance vector* results from the described assessment options that are feasible for SMEs (see Figure 4.6).

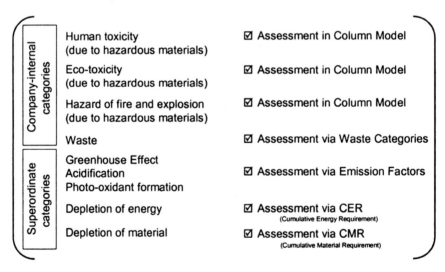

Fig. 4.6. Environmental performance vector in the EPM-KOMPAS

---

[12] For selected raw materials and energy carriers, the CER and CMR factors were retrieved from the GEMIS database (www.oeko.de/service/gemis/).

Filled in with values, the vector can assume a form as shown in figure 4.1. With this multi-dimensional result, a company now has to decide between the individual impact categories. This necessitates determining whether a dominant category (e.g. energy requirement) exists for the SME. However, it can also be of interest to examine whether a master parameter is relevant to several categories (for this example, the THERM ZINC DUST VARNISH material, which appears in three impact categories of the environmental performance vector as presenting a high or medium hazard). Another decision needs to be made in terms of the environmental and economic dimensions, expressed as quantities/ volumes and costs.[13] Should the master parameter with the highest costs or the highest quantities/ volumes be considered?

Company-internal categories	Human toxicity (due to hazardous materials)	✦ High hazard: FAN-EP Hardener
		✦ Medium hazard: THERM Zinc dust varnish
		✦ Medium to Low hazard: CHING-PUR Surface coating
	Eco-toxicity (due to hazardous materials)	✦ Very High hazard: CHING PUR Surface coating
		✦ Medium hazard: THERM Zinc dust varnish
	Hazard of fire and explosion (due to hazardous materials)	✦ High hazard: THERM Zinc dust varnish
		✦ Medium hazard: CHING PUR Surface coating
	Waste	✦ Sludges from paint or varnish containing organic solvents or other dangerous substances
Superordinate categories	Greenhouse Effect	✦ 29,347.45 kg CO_2
	Depletion of energy	✦ Highest CER Value: Aluminium
	Depletion of material	✦ Highest CMR Value: Sheet Steel

Fig. 4.7. Assessed environmental performance vector in the EPM-KOMPAS

This assessment method serves to reduce complexity by focussing on a few master parameters and complies with the motto: *Not complete, but significant!*

---

[13] Naturally, an overlapping of environmental and economic action potentials is ideal; this applies to cases where a cost-relevant aspect is also environmentally dominant in several categories.

4.4.4 Steps 3 and 4: Identifying Performance Drivers and Determining Objectives

In *Step 3*, the cause analysis is used (see Figure 4.8), which assists in investigating the causative agents of master parameters by way of analysing their drivers within the company.

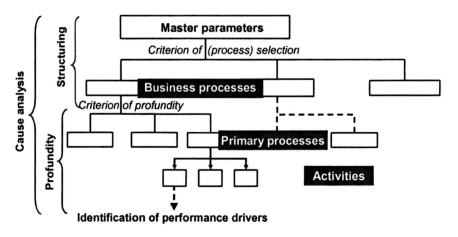

Fig. 4.8. Cause analysis – from master parameter to performance driver

In the EPM-KOMPAS, this material flow analysis for identifying cause-and-effect chains is backed by impulse questions and tips and enables companies to trace the input/ output paths (raw materials, auxiliary materials, hazardous materials, waste, etc.) across the company and back to the locations from where they originated or were caused. The cause analysis can conclude on a very high aggregation level (e.g. process groups); however, it is practical to subject it to a more in-depth analysis in order to reach conclusive results, so that the performance driver along with the linked (sub)process become evident. This approach complies with the motto: *Transparency via logical structure!*

The material flow analysis conducted by a company identifies corporate master parameters and their performance drivers and points out action areas for effective environmental protection. In *Step 4*, (environmental performance) objectives should be defined for each individual action area. This systematic assistance in the EPM-KOMPAS supports SMEs in regards to the issue of the objective setting process, which is problematic for them, since project experience gathered with practice partners as well as research results show that companies face great difficulties when developing environmental objectives, proceed in an unsystematic manner and according to their own statements, lack the criteria for developing environmental objectives (Ankele/ Kottmann, 2000).

4.4.5 Steps 5 and 6: Establishing a Process Balance and Selecting Measures

In order to implement this objective for the master parameter, a list of measures can be created subsequent to the process material flow analysis (*Step 5*), which comprises master parameters and performance drivers. To this end, a process balance is established for the relevant (sub)processes in period t_1, which indicates the input and output materials of the involved (sub)processes, interdependencies in regards to the measures to be taken as well as both the beneficial and detrimental side effects related to changes in the process. At the same time, this enhances the transparency of the internal (corporate) material flows and the relevance and completeness of the company's environmental data. Subsequently, this information can be used in *Step 6* to decide on concrete measures. In this context, a calculation method is integrated into the tool that enables an advance assessment of the planned measures with respect to their economic benefit value.

Up to this step, considerations focus on the goal of improving the environmental performance of a process/ the company, whereas economic objectives take a back seat. Thus, only environmental objectives are at the forefront up to step 6. However, each measure should, of course, be economically feasible. To ensure this, the EPM-KOMPAS takes recourse to the classic assessment method for measures, namely investment appraisal. Therefore, the "net present value method" is integrated into the tool. Companies are encouraged to prepare an accurate breakdown of inpayment and outpayment and conduct an assessment of measures.

Only measures with a net present value ≥ 0 are explicitly recommended for implementtation. With net present values < 0, companies are faced with the decision of taking a measure despite its lack of economic feasibility. Strategic or synergetic effects in the sense of effects on other sectors may speak in favour of doing so. If, however, a company is forced to take such measures (e.g. due to legal requirements, etc.), it knows whether the investment will result in future inpayment and outpayment.

4.4.6 Step 7: Carrying Out the Environmental Success Breakdown and Variance Analysis

Within the scope of company practice, identifying the effectiveness of measures and the achieved results and success is more important than ever. In order to determine the success characteristics of the environmental success after carrying out a measure, the environmental success breakdown method is used (see Figure 4.9.). For this, the total difference is broken down according to predefined parameters in order to map the original environmental success achieved by the company. By way of impulse questions, the split-offs regarding external and non-intended result components are stored in the tool. The environmental success breakdown in *Step 6* analyses the success of environmental measures regarding:

- success components outside the chosen system boundary: to separate them and hence, to analyse only the remaining success that is included in the system boundary;
- non-intended success components like accidents and disasters influencing the intended success either by improving or deteriorating and therefore, must be separated;
- variances in production (or equal corporate reference values) to clarify which component of success is due to a higher production level and has to be separated to analyse only the efficiency of the measure itself;
- the efficiency of the measure with assuming a constant production level.

These split-offs in the environmental success breakdown were selected according to the motto: *Not too complex, but understandable!*

4.4.7 In Detail: The Environmental Success Breakdown

The environmental success breakdown method was developed along the lines of the breakdown method of economic success and analyses the results in regards to their causative agents and sources within a company.

The practical application of the environmental success breakdown has made it evident that a precise cause analysis is a prerequisite for the successful generation of measures. Adopting the principle of structuring the breakdown of economic success into success analysis and success control, the first step of the environmental success breakdown can be viewed as a cause analysis (see chapter 4.4.4). This cause analysis serves the purpose of researching which cause-and-effect links exist between master parameters and performance drivers at the process level (see Figure 4.8.).

The thus identified performance drivers form the basis for generating objectives and measures. The actual success breakdown and variance analyses are then conducted subsequent to the implementation of the measure(s) (see Figure 4.9).

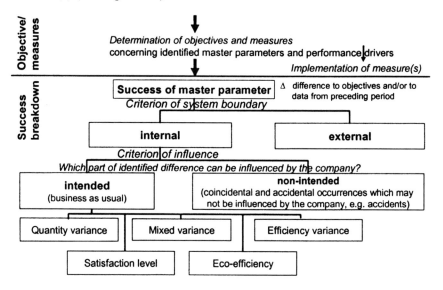

Fig. 4.9. Environmental success breakdown – from measure to improved environmental performance

Separating internal and external success components (e.g. due to outsourcing) is practical and feasible for companies. The (remaining) success component within the selected system boundary must then be examined in regards to the question of whether, and to what extent, the company was able to influence the result of the master parameter. In the case of uncontrollable or unintended incidents (events not under the influence or control of the company), actual or estimated pollution/reduction values can be shown here. The analyses of the remaining intended success comprises the classic economic variance analyses (quantity, mixed and efficiency variances), the calculation of the degree to which objectives were met and an examination of eco-efficiency changes.

Please refer to the case study in chapter 6 for an environmental success breakdown application example and the underlying equations. The reason for selecting the differentiated-cumulative variance analysis method lies in the fact that it completely breaks down the total variance into primary variances, i.e. quantity and efficiency variances, and into higher-order variances, i.e. mixed variance (Geskes, 2000).

Moreover, the differenttiated-cumulative variance analysis method eliminates the issue of the sequence of quantity/ volume and efficiency variances split-off (as is the case with, e.g., cumulative variance analysis).

As shown in figure 4.10., splitting off the quantity variance prior to the efficiency variance can yield different results than splitting off the efficiency variance before the quantity variance.

Therefore, in order to avoid this and in view of the practicability requirement of the EPM-KOMPAS, the differentiated-cumulative variance analysis method is used (see Figure 4.10.).

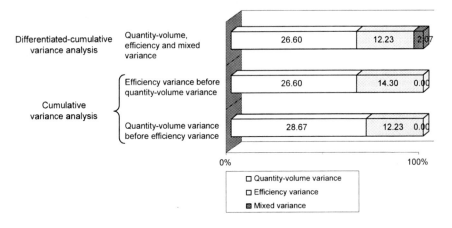

Fig. 4.10. Results according to the differentiated cumulative variance analysis as compared with two possible results of the cumulative variance analysis.

4.4.8 Step 8: Review of Actions and Objectives

In the concluding *Step 8*, companies can review their objectives and derive action recommendations for the next periods and/or revise their objectives and define new ones. Options include starting over with Step 1 of the tool (e.g., because the company was able to already identify new, significant environmental aspects when first using the EPM-KOMPAS) or maintaining the master parameters and going back to Step 4 while taking into account the findings from Step 7 and the action recommendations from Step 8. This complies with the motto: *Not rigid, but flexible!* Thus, Step 8 concludes the familiar plan-do-check-act management cycle and triggers a continuous improvement process.

4.5 Practical Application: A Case Study

4.5.1 Data Collection

Cast Iron GmbH can utilise comprehensive paper-based information, mainly in the form of purchasing, accounting, warehouse and production documents as well as some measurements that were taken once to twelve times per year, depending on the material. Based on this available data and by way of impulse questions concerning the relevant internal and external stakeholders and environmental issues, master parameters were determined with a qualitative assessment method for/ in co-operation with Cast Iron GmbH in Step 2 of the EPM-KOMPAS. "What we do not have is a hazardous material register and input/output balances, the reason being that we are simply somewhat too small for that. It is true that, as a foundry, our facilities require official approval, which results in an information and documentation obligation towards the authorities. However, this does not necessitate a requirement for precise input/ output balances" (Managing Director, Cast Iron GmbH).

4.5.2 Stakeholder Analysis

The most important stakeholders for Cast Iron GmbH comprise insurance companies (on the grounds of malfunctions/ accidents), environmental authorities (due to co-operation and reporting obligations) and, in addition, legislative bodies. Residents are viewed as a special stakeholders in regards to possible noise pollution, and for the customers of Cast Iron GmbH, environmental protection is a given: "Reputable customers expect environmental protection to be one of our safety and quality features" (Managing Director, Cast Iron GmbH). Moreover, concrete questions were asked with respect to areas in which future improvements and/ or changes were desired. In this context, it could be ascertained that, due to internal monitoring, the effect of dust and noise pollution on the residents does not constitute a problem area. However, it is a primary objective of Cast Iron GmbH to close internal material cycles and thus reduce waste. Reductions are also desired in terms of energy consumption and air emissions. In conclusion, it can be stated that the master parameters of Cast Iron GmbH in regards to this full EPM-KOMPAS run are located in the following areas: the amount of generated used sand and dross and the use of natural gas. A decision was made for the *used foundry sand* as master parameter.

4.5.3 Cause Analysis

In Step 3 of the EPM-KOMPAS, the corresponding performance driver for the master parameter used foundry sand was identified via a cause analysis. A company-wide analysis across the individual process levels and down to the location of origin demonstrated that the silicate bonded portion of the pit-iron sand deployed in the sub-process *core making* is the origin of the used foundry sand at Cast Iron GmbH (see Figure 4.11.). Thus, the use of *silicate*[14] could be identified as the performance driver.

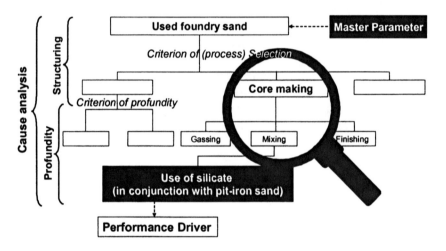

Fig. 4.11. Cause analysis with master parameter and performance driver at Cast Iron GmbH

After processing steps 1 to 3 of the EPM-KOMPAS, it became apparent that the master parameter used foundry sand should be influenced in a further environmental objective. Moreover, it is known that, as the causative agent of the master parameter used foundry sand, the performance driver silicate in the core making process has to be formulated for this purpose. Therefore, in step 4, Cast Iron GmbH formulates an objective for this action area. An objective for the master parameter used foundry sand in Step 4 of the EPM-KOMPAS was formulated to the effect that the level of the previous year should be maintained.

Narrowing down the subject to the sub-process core making then enabled a precise material flow analysis in Step 5. The first prerequisite for this was the creation of a process flow chart by Cast Iron GmbH in order to

---

[14] Chemical substance used in core making.

be able to estimate the extent, inputs and outputs as well as inter-dependencies of the process. This was facilitated by the fact that a sub-process actually represents a system or subsystem within a company.

Next, the material and energy flows were recorded in detail, based on the sub-process core making. "A problem lies with compiling the data specific to the equipment and machinery, since in this area, the equipment as a whole plays a role and we do not collect data in this way. There is only a limited number of machines with hour meters or similar devices installed on them; e.g., our welding furnaces are of course equipped with hour meters for the welding torches, but not for the core casting machine. We have determined the connected loads and attempted to establish a certain rate of use in co-operation with our engineers. In regards to air consumption – usually, the foundry has high air requirements – matters are even more complex. In this area, we cannot specify the exact amount of air consumed by a specific machine. This would only be possible by deploying sophisticated measuring technology." (Managing Director, Cast Iron GmbH)

The process balances for 1999 (see Table 4.2), 2000 (see Table 4.3) and 2001 (see Table 4.4) were created by using available measurement data and calculating the implicit and explicit consumption by way of technical specifications or estimates based on equivalence numbers.[15] For Cast Iron GmbH, determining the number of cores and casts produced per year would have required too much time and effort. The air and energy consumption involved in core shooting as well as the percentage of rejects were calculated based on the technical machine specifications and supple-mented with estimates.

Table 4.2. 1999: Core Making Process Balance of Cast Iron GmbH

Input 1999			
Category	Name	Properties	Quantity/Volume
Materials	Pit-iron Sand	Natural mineral, not harmful to water	80.01 t [a]
	Silicate	Sodium silicate, water hazard class 1	1.76 t [a]
	CO_2	Not harmful to water	3.46 t [a]

---

[15] The corresponding data quality is identified in the process balances.

Table 4.2. (Cont.)

Materials	Ethanol	VbF (German Flammable Liquids Ordinance) class B, water hazard class 1, highly flammable	487.74 kg [a]
	Graphite Powder		60.18 kg [a]
Air	Compressed Air		1,023 m³ [c]
Energy	Electricity		3,068 kWh [b]
Output 1999			
Products	Cores		16,835 pcs. [b]
Waste	Waste not otherwise specified; wastes from casting of non-ferrous pieces, here: used foundry sand	Supervision-requiring	129.80 t [a]

a Measured
b Calculated
c Estimated

Table 4.3. 2000: Core Making Process Balance of Cast Iron GmbH

Input 2000			
Category	Name	Properties	Quantity/Volume
Materials	Pit-iron Sand	Natural mineral, not harmful to water	134.92 t [a]
	Silicate	Sodium silicate, water hazard class 1	5.07 t [a]
	CO_2	Not harmful to water	4.88 t [a]
	Ethanol	VbF (German Flammable Liquids Ordinance) class B, water hazard class 1, highly flammable	731.61 kg [a]
	Graphite Powder		40.12 kg [a]
Air	Compressed Air		1,023 m³ [c]
Energy	Electricity		3,839 kWh [b]

Table 4.3. (Cont.)

Output 2000			
Products	Cores		28,320 pcs. [b]
Waste	Waste not otherwise specified; wastes from casting of non-ferrous pieces, here: used foundry sand	Supervision-requiring	157.34 t [a]

a Measured
b Calculated
c Estimated

Table 4.4. 2001: Core Making Process Balance of Cast Iron GmbH

Input 2001			
Category	Name	Properties	Quantity/ Volume
Materials	Pit-iron Sand	Natural mineral, not harmful to water	157.73 t [a]
	Silicate	Sodium silicate, water hazard class 1	5.66 t [a]
	CO_2	Not harmful to water	5.43 t [a]
	Ethanol	VbF (German Flammable Liquids Ordinance) class B, water hazard class 1, highly flammable	731.61 kg [a]
	Graphite Powder		80.24 kg [a]
Air	Compressed Air		1,023 m³ [c]
Energy	Electricity		4,858 kWh [b]
Output 2001			
Products	Cores		33,119 pcs. [b]
Waste	Waste not otherwise specified; wastes from casting of non-ferrous pieces, here: used foundry sand	Supervision-requiring	198.24 t [a]

a Measured
b Calculated
c Estimated

The analyses in Step 7 of the EPM-KOMPAS[16] are to be based on the year 2000 values as objective/planned values in comparison to the actual values for 2001. These analyses and split-offs of the environmental success were based on the following equations, with the "ACTUAL" index applicable to the collected quantity/ volume data for period 2 (i.e. *after* implementing the measure) and the "PLAN" index applicable to the specified target quantities/ volumes or the quantities/ volumes in period 1 (i.e. *before* implementing the measure) as the basis of comparison. The environmental success is calculated with equation 5.1:

$$\text{Environmental Success}_{\text{MASTER PARAMETER}} = \qquad (5.1)$$
$$\text{Environmental Performance Master Parameter}_{\text{PLAN}} -$$
$$\text{Environmental Performance Master Parameter}_{\text{ACTUAL}}$$

If external success (i.e. results) components are split off, the following equation 5.2 applies to the remaining internal success (i.e. results)[17]:

$$\text{Internal Success}_{\text{MASTER PARAMETER}} = \qquad (5.2)$$
$$\text{Environmental Success}_{\text{MASTER PARAMETER}} -$$
$$(\text{External Success}_{\text{MASTER PARAMETER}})$$

If additional non-intended success (i.e. results) components exist, the intended success remains as calculated via equation 5.3:

$$\text{Intended Success}_{\text{MASTER PARAMETER}} = \qquad (5.3)$$
$$\text{Internal Success}_{\text{MASTER PARAMETER}} -$$
$$(\text{Non-intended Success}_{\text{MASTER PARAMETER}})$$

If external success and/ or non-intended success exists, the axiomatic environmental performance of Master Parameter $_{\text{ACTUAL}}$ (i.e. output quantity) also changes, since these components are separately examined and split off (because they would distort the actual result). Thus, the following applies to Master Parameter $_{\text{ACTUAL, NEW}}$ (see equation 5.4):

$$\text{Environmental Performance Master Parameter}_{\text{ACTUAL, NEW}} = \quad (5.4)$$
$$\text{Environmental Performance Master Parameter}_{\text{ACTUAL}} +$$
$$(\text{External Success}_{\text{MASTER PARAMETER}}) +$$
$$(\text{Non-intended Success}_{\text{MASTER PARAMETER}})$$

Thus, the intended success is the object of the variance analyses. Conducting the variance analysis now requires utilising a reference quantity

---

[16] At Cast Iron GmbH, measures relevant to the project EPM-KOMPAS were not determined or implemented.

[17] The brackets serve the mathematical function of enclosing the positive or negative external success (result).

that corresponds in quantity/ volume to the output quantity of the master parameter. A quantity value that has a significant connection to the selected performance driver and the identified master parameter should be chosen as a reference value (e.g. production quantity/ volume, type representative, etc.).

The quantity variance to be split off indicates the portion of the environmental success that is attributable to an increase or decrease in the reference quantity, i.e., the quantity variance indicates which portion of the environmental success was determined by, e.g., increased production.

For the purpose of breaking down this environmental success[18], the input quantity of pit-iron sand is utilised as a reference quantity that corresponds in quantity/ volume to the output quantity of the master parameter used foundry sand. Thus, the following equation applies to splitting off the quantity variance (see equation 5.5):

$$\text{Quantity Variance} = \text{Environmental Performance Master} \qquad (5.5)$$
$$\text{Parameter}_{PLAN} -$$
$$(\text{Reference Quantity Volume}_{ACTUAL} \times \text{Eco-efficiency}_{PLAN})$$

In this context, the following equation applies to Eco-efficiency $_{PLAN}$: [19]

$$\text{Eco-efficiency}_{PLAN} = \qquad (5.6)$$
$$\text{Environmental Performance Master Parameter}_{PLAN} /$$
$$\text{Reference Value}_{PLAN}$$

The efficiency variance describes the portion of the result that is attributable to the effectiveness of the measure; thus, it describes the environmental efficiency of the measure. Equation 5.7 appears as follows:

$$\text{Efficiency Variance} = \text{Environmental Performance Master} \qquad (5.7)$$
$$\text{parameter}_{PLAN} -$$
$$(\text{Reference Value}_{PLAN} \times \text{Eco-efficiency}_{ACTUAL})$$

Eco-efficiency $_{ACTUAL}$ is calculated as follows:

$$\text{Eco-efficiency}_{ACTUAL} = \qquad (5.8)$$
$$\text{Environmental Performance Master Parameter}_{ACTUAL,\ NEW} /$$
$$\text{Reference Value}_{ACTUAL}$$

---

[18] Following the concept of success as perceived in the economic/ business administration field, environmental success can assume both positive and negative values; see chapter 3.

[19] The output quantity of Master Parameter $_{PLAN}$ does not change if external and non-intended success exist.

In regards to the mixed variance resulting from the remaining variance components that were not subject to a more detailed analysis and cannot be attributed to a specific variance cause (Coenenberg, 2003), the following equation forms the basis for the analysis:

$$\text{Mixed Variance} = (\text{Eco-efficiency}_{\text{PLAN}} - \text{Eco-efficiency}_{\text{ACTUAL}}) \quad (5.9)$$
$$\text{x}$$
$$(\text{Reference Value}_{\text{ACTUAL}} - \text{Reference Value}_{\text{PLAN}})$$

The degree to which objectives were met is calculated as follows by using the environmental success breakdown and, in this context, does not refer to the output quantity/ environmental performance of Master Parameter $_{\text{ACTUAL}}$, as would be the case without applying the environmental success breakdown, but with linking Reference Value $_{\text{PLAN}}$ with Eco-efficiency $_{\text{ACTUAL}}$, which contains the adjusted environmental performance of Master Parameter $_{\text{ACTUAL, NEW}}$ if external and non-intended success exist:

$$\text{Satisfaction level} = \quad (5.10)$$
$$\text{Environmental Performance Master Parameter}_{\text{PLAN}} /$$
$$\text{Reference Value}_{\text{PLAN}} \text{ x Eco-efficiency}_{\text{ACTUAL}}$$

These equations, when applied to the pertinent Cast Iron GmbH data, yield the results shown in table 4.5.

Table 4.5. 2000/ 2001 Outcome of environmental success breakdown and variance analyses at Cast Iron GmbH

Environmental Success	157.34 t – 198.24 t	- 40.9 t
Quantity Variance	157.34 t – 157.73 t x 1.16617 t/t	- 26.6 t
Efficiency Variance	157.34 t – 134.92 t x 1.25683 t/t	- 12.23 t
Mixed Variance	(1.16617 t/t - 1.25683 t/t) x (157.73 t - 134.92 t)	- 2.07 t
Eco-efficiency Change	1.16617 t/t ÷ 1.25683 t/t	- 0.0906 t/t
Satisfaction Level	157.34 t ÷ (157.73 t x 1.25683 t/t)	92 %

Figure 4.12. illustrates how these results are classified into the environmental success breakdown diagram:

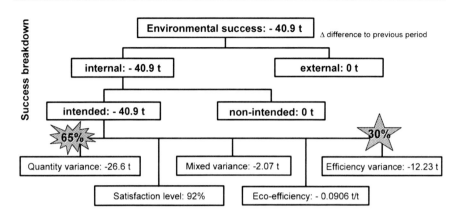

Fig. 4.12. Results of environmental success breakdown

Based on the finding that a large portion (65%) of the negative result is attributable to an increase in the reference quantity and only 30% are rooted in environmental inefficiencies, the company can draw conclusions in Step 8 of the EPM-KOMPAS and derive action recommendations for the next periods and/ or define new objectives.

4.6 Strategic Environmental Management and the EPM-KOMPAS Options

The EPM-KOMPAS tool described here aims at supporting SMEs in their strategic actions and in the integration of their environmental aspects into the internal decision-making process, since SMEs have an unquestionably high avoidance potential in regards to environmental pollution and the requirements on the part of their clients and major customers necessitate exploring, in co-operation with SMEs, options for mobilising their strategic environment-oriented policies and supporting their efforts. In this context, a management tool has to be offered that takes into account the problems, that arises for SMEs in regards to strategic environment-oriented information, decision-making and that offers solutions. This tool then has a decision supporting, not merely a reporting function. The EPM-KOMPAS was developed in full awareness of the fact that strategic environment-oriented management is increasingly important for SMEs in order to secure a company's continued existence in the long term. The beginning for this is a strategic analysis.

This analysis serves the purposes of researching and collecting information with respect to starting points for strategic measures and for a successful strategy formulation. In order to conduct this analysis in SMEs, a decision tool must offer support in

1. identifying the strengths and weaknesses of a company;
2. identifying the opportunities and threats within the company's sphere; and
3. determining strategies and objectives. (Günther and Kaulich, 2003)

Moreover, such a decision tool should have the capability of offering the "right" information at the "right" time in the "right" form, since it can be viewed as a management subsystem which, by providing information, supports companies in their efforts to optimally meet their objectives (Horváth, 2002). Thus, companies can adapt to changing conditions within their spheres ("ability to adapt"), co-ordinate internal actions and decisions ("ability to co-ordinate") and respond to changes ("ability to react") (Horváth, 2002). As a result, two additional requirements for a decision tool can be indicated:

4. supporting the process of collecting and structuring information; and
5. supporting decision-making in order to develop strengths, minimise weaknesses, seize opportunities and avoid threats. (Günther and Kaulich, 2003)

In the EPM-KOMPAS, these identified requirements were taken into account particularly for SMEs (see Table 4.6), in order to support them on their path.

Table 4.6. Strategic options facilitated by the EPM-KOMPAS (Günther/ Kaulich, 2003)

1.	Support in identifying the strengths and weaknesses of a company.	
✓	Step 2	By selecting the master parameters to be improved and based on the "not complete, but significant" motto, complexity is reduced to the significant environmental aspects of SMEs, resulting in an identification of strengths and weaknesses.
✓ ✓	Step 7 Step 8	By carrying out a success breakdown and conducting action and objectives reviews, the achieved improvements in regards to the identified strengths/weaknesses (embodied by the master parameters) can be adjusted to the objectives and initial data, in order to be able to select in step 2, new master parameters to be improved for the next period, if necessary.

Table 4.6. (Cont.)

2.	Support in identifying the opportunities and threats within the company's sphere.	
✓	Step 2	In the qualitative assessment and by way of impulse questions, SMEs are made aware of the exemplary interests of relevant internal/external stakeholders (e.g. via questions regarding major customers or legal requirements) and/or current environmental topics (potential sources of risk), the examination of which assists in minimising threats and identifying opportunities.
✓	Step 6	SMEs are supported via impulse questions concerning incentive measures, development programmes, grants and subsidies for measures as well as general legal requirements (e.g. limits).
3.	Support in determining strategies and objectives.	
✓	Step 2	The prioritisation of the significant environmental aspects of SMEs by way of environmental assessment and complexity reduction via the subsequent selection of master parameters enables SMEs to focus on the essential, i.e. efficient action areas, develop strategies for influencing these areas and determine objectives (avoiding taking action for the sake of taking action in favour of setting a strategic course).
✓	Step 4	Each of the results gathered in the previous steps facilitate the determination of objectives in SMEs and thus enables them to specify objectives for the selected master parameters.
4.	Support in the process of collecting and structuring information.	
✓	Step 1	The recording of internal data regarding significant environmental aspects initiates the collection and structuring of environment-oriented data and/or clarifies where in the company such data is already available/still needs to be obtained.
✓	Step 3	The cause analysis structures and visualises existing company data by establishing a causative link between a master parameter and its performance driver(s).

Table 4.6. (Cont.)

5.	Support with decision-making process in order to develop strengths, minimise weaknesses, seize opportunities and avoid threats.
✓ Step 2 ✓ Step 4 ✓ Step 6 ✓ Step 7	The tool supports SMEs in preparing and making decisions by way of quantitative and qualitative assessment in regards to the selection of master parameters, support in determining objectives for these master parameters, integration of impulse questions and calculation methods with respect to the investment decision-making process, and implementation of the success breakdown for deriving action recommendations.

4.7 Outlook

Due to its comprehensive approach, the EPM-KOMPAS can greatly influence the decision-making, planning, control and monitoring processes in a company. Thus, the aim should be an integration into the existing decision processes at a company, since the measured environmental performance of a company/ a process/ a product form the basis for entre-preneurial and business decisions. On the basis of the driver analysis and environmental success breakdown, direct control and influence on the environmental performance should be possible. An analysis of these driver values represents a structured method for decomposing the data provided by the eco-balance and other ecology-oriented tools into controllable driver and influence values, i.e. reference points for decision-making.

References

Ankele K, Kottmann H (2000) Ökologische Zielfindung im Rahmen des Umwelt-managements. no 147/00, Berlin

Coenenberg, A-G (2003) Kostenrechnung und Kostenanalyse. vol 5, Stuttgart

Encyclopaedia Britannica (ed) (2000) Encyclopaedia Britannica Premium Service. (URL: http://www.brittanica.com)

European Parliament and the Council of the European Union (2001) Regulation (EC) no 761/01 of the European Parliament and the council of the European Union of 19 March 2001 allowing voluntary participation by organisations in a Community eco-management and audit scheme (EMAS). Official Journal of the European Communities 44:L114

Federal Environmental Ministry, Federal Environmental Agency (ed) (1997) A guide to corporate environmental indicators. Bonn Berlin

Federal Environmental Agency (ed) (1999) Valuation as an element of Life Cycle Assessment. no 92/99, Berlin (only in German)

Federal Environmental Agency (ed) (2002) Life Cycle Assessment for Beverage Packaging Systems II / Phase 2, no 51/02, Berlin (only in German)

Freeman R E (1984) Strategic Management – A Stakeholder Approach. Marsfield Massachusetts

Geskes S (2000) Methoden der deckungsbeitragsorientierten Abweichungs-analyse: Information, Anreiz und Kontrolle in Unternehmungen. Frankfurt/ Main

Gleich R (2001) Das System des Performance Measurement. Theoretisches Grundkonzept, Entwicklungs- und Anwendungsstand. Munich

Günther E, Kaulich S (2003) EPM-KOMPAS: An instrument to control environ-mental performance in SMES - from a strategic point of view. In: ERP Environment (ed) The 2003 Business Strategy and the Environment Conference. Conference Proceedings, Leicester, pp 165 - 172

Horváth P (2002) Controlling. 8th edn, Munich

International Organisation for Standardisation (ISO) (ed) (2000) Environmental Management – Life Cycle Assessment – Life Cycle Impact Assessment, ISO 14042:2000, Geneva

International Organisation for Standardisation (ISO) (ed) (1999) Environmental Management – Environmental Performance Evaluation – Guidelines, ISO 14031:1999. Geneva

Kottman H, Loew T, Clausen J (1999) Umweltmanagement mit Kennzahlen. Munich

Lampert H, Althammer J (2001) Lehrbuch der Sozialpolitik. 6th edn, Berlin

Lankoski L (2000) Determinants of Environmental Profit. An analysis of the firm-level relationship between environmental performance and economic performance. Doctoral Dissertation, Helsinki

Schaltegger S, Wagner M, Wehrmeyer W (2001) The Relationship between the Environmental and Economic Performance of Firms. What does theory propose and what does empirical evidence tell us? In: GMI 34, pp 95-108

Stahlmann V, Clausen J (2000) Umweltleistung von Unternehmen, Von der Öko-Effizienz zur Öko-Effektivität. Wiesbaden

Stefan U et al. (1995) Nationale und europäische Umwelthaftung – Eine Hürde für den Mittelstand? no 65 NF, Stuttgart

Steinle C, Reiter F (ed) (2002) Ökologieorientiertes Anreiz- und Entwicklungsmanagement für mittelständische Unternehmen. In 5 Schritten zum erfolgreichen Umweltmanagement. In: Initiativen zum Umweltschutz, no 48, Berlin

Wagner M (2003) How does it pay to be green? An Analysis of the Relationship between Environmental and Economic Performance at the Firm Level and the Influence of Corporate Environmental Strategy Choice. Dissertation. Marburg, Germany

5 Integrated Controlling Based on Material and Energy Flow Analysis – A Case Study in Foundry Industries

Christoph Lange, André Kuchenbuch

Christoph Lange, Chair of Environmental Management and Controlling, University of Duisburg-Essen, Germany
E-Mail: c.lange@uni-essen.de

André Kuchenbuch, Chair of Environmental Management and Controlling, University of Duisburg-Essen, BehrHella Thermocontrol GmbH, Lippstadt, Germany
E-Mail: a.kuchenbuch@cityweb.de

5.1 Introduction

The basis of the following paper is the project entitled "Development of an Integrated Controlling Concept Based on a Process-oriented Costing System with Regard to Optimised Material and Energy Flows in Iron, Steel and Malleable Iron Foundries" (INPROCESS), sponsored by the *Bundesministerium für Bildung und Forschung* (German Federal Ministry of Education and Research). The project is an interdisciplinary research project that aims at creating practically-oriented controlling tools in a sustainable development context.

5.1.1 The INPROCESS Project

Project Members

In addition to the core project team, project partners comprise the German Foundry Association, the Chair of Environmental Management and Controlling at the University of Duisburg-Essen/ Germany (Essen Campus), the German Institute of Foundry Technology, the ARÖW – Gesellschaft für Arbeits-, Reorganisations- und Ökologische Wirtschaftsberatung mbH (a business consultants network specialised in occupational, reorganisation and ecological consulting) and nine foundries, in which the content-related focuses of the project (material flow analyses, process-oriented environmental activity based costing, integrated performance indicator systems) were examined in the form of case studies.[1]

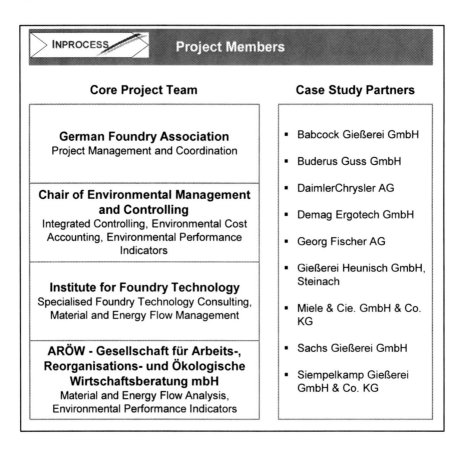

Fig. 5.1. Inprocess project members[2]

---

[1] See Lange et al. 2002; Lange and Kuchenbuch 2003a, p. 26 et seq.; Kuchenbuch et al. 2004, pp. 24-29

[2] Source: Lange and Kuchenbuch 2003, p. 27, Remarks: The authors would like to thank all the participants of the INPROCESS project, particularly the co-operating practice partners, without whom the project results would not have been possible.

Presentation of the Problem

In the face of increasing environmental pollution, scarcity of resources and an intensified competitive atmosphere, foundries are being challenged by increasingly dynamic structures and processes:

- Factors related to the environment are continually gaining in importance, be they linked to the obligation to meet legal stipulated requirements or to voluntary compliance with specific threshold values for the purpose of boosting the company's image or in anticipation of future developments, etc.
- The pressure to reduce costs makes it essential for the foundries to optimise their material and energy flows.
- To this end, both cost-effectiveness as well as ecological efficiency have to be ensured and monitorable.

However, the required co-ordination, planning and controlling run into difficulties, since conventional costing and controlling systems do not allow any integrated control of the various, thematically different areas.

Objective

The objective of this project is to unite, for the benefit of the sector, two essential task areas within the scope of decisions that are environmentally related and based on the principle of sustainable management:

1. Process-oriented controlling based on material flow and energy management, comprising the following tasks:
   - Identification, recording and documentation of the material and energy flows
   - Identification of the savings potentials for the most significant resource consumption areas
   - Outline and description of the measures for implementing the savings potentials

   The resultant findings and identified measures for reducing the usage of resources are prepared in a way that enables the foundries to independently realise corresponding improvements. To support them in this, extensive guidelines will be created within the scope of the project.

2. Derivation of a requirements profile for the expansion of costing systems in regards to environmental protection, allowing for optimised material and energy flows as a component of integrated controlling.

   On the basis of the results of the analyses, the aforementioned guidelines will be provided for the purpose of planning, controlling and monitoring both the economic and ecological objectives within the framework of an integrated controlling system.

5.1.2 Basics of Integrated Controlling

Constantly accelerating changes on the markets associated with a growing segmentation of customer groups, rising innovation rates and accordingly shorter product life cycles result in a rapid change in the competitive environment of companies. For the most part, only those companies that offer customised, exceptionally innovative, qualitatively high-quality and environmentally-friendly products and services produced with the use of few resources can remain competitive over the long-term.[3] Foundries also have to address these changes and must gear their management and performance processes towards market demands.

This necessitates a broadening of the focus of the primarily company-internal – in part also only accounting-oriented – approach to controlling by incorporating perspectives that extend beyond the company boundaries.[4] In addition to the expansion of this approach, an orientation on the guiding principle of sustainable development requires the creation of a multi-criteria objective system that comprises not only economic, but ecological and social objectives as well.

In the context of the conducted project, integrated controlling can be defined as a management subprocess, essentially pertaining to the (company-internal) business processes as well as the (inter-company) value-added chain, for co-ordinating management activities on all decision-making levels of the company. Controlling should thus be primarily geared towards the company-internal interfaces (e.g. within and between business processes, departments and divisions).[5] Furthermore, it should increasingly provide the information that is requested by those stakeholders (e.g. customers, authorities, suppliers, employees, residents) who are deemed strategically relevant.

To implement the concept of integrated controlling, the following potential expansion stages can be derived.[6]

---

[3] See Schaefer 2001, p. 1

[4] See Lange et al. 2001, p. 75; Lange and Martensen 2003

[5] See Lange et al. 2001, p. 75

[6] For more detailed information on the concept of integrated controlling see Lange et al. 2001, Schaefer 2001; Daldrup 2002, pp. 9-32.

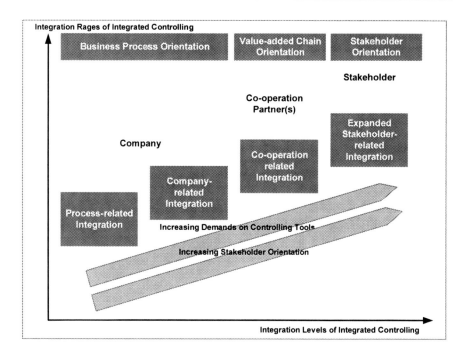

Fig. 5.2. Expansion stages of integrated controlling[7]

As an example, the following table illustrates the effects that the different expansion stages of integrated controlling have on the company's objective system.

Table 5.1. Examples of the expansion stages of integrated controlling[8]

Process and Company-related Integration	Co-operation-related Integration	Expanded Stakeholder-related Integration
• Expansion of objective system via the addition of requirements of e.g. employees, management	• Expansion of objective system via the addition of requirements of e.g. customers, suppliers	• Expansion of objective system via the addition of requirements of e.g. residents, authorities

[7] Source: Lange and Kuchenbuch 2003, p. 27
[8] Source: Lange and Kuchenbuch 2003, p. 27; Kuchenbuch et al. 2004, p. 25

Table 5.1. (Cont.)

• Possible objectives: identification of cost reduction potentials, increase in transparency regarding material and energy flows, substitution of noxious materials	• Possible objectives: establishment of development partnerships, reduction in product development times	• Possible objectives: reduction of noise and dust emissions

The objective of integrated controlling can thus be seen as the support of management in the formulation and communication of a company policy that addresses the interests of preferably all stakeholders deemed to be strategically relevant. This also includes the provision of information that enables all management levels to implement a sustainable company management, with process integration at the forefront of this contribution.

5.2 Phase Model for Introducing Integrated Controlling in Foundry Companies

Based on the above-mentioned necessity for a re-orientation of controlling, a phase model for the foundry sector was developed within the scope of the underlying research project. The phase model was intended to serve as a means of orientation for the companies to assist them in adapting their internal information procurement and decision-making support processes to the changed market conditions. In this context, it was ensured that the recommended tools were based on information and tools already existing in the foundries, in order to keep reorganisation expenses and efforts as low as possible and thus increase acceptance of the proposed concept.

The following diagram provides an overview of the phases of the model:[9]

---

[9] For more on the specific content of the individual tools/ phases of this model, see Kuchenbuch et al. 2003; Lange and Kuchenbuch 2003; Lange and Kuchenbuch 2003a; Lange et al. 2003.

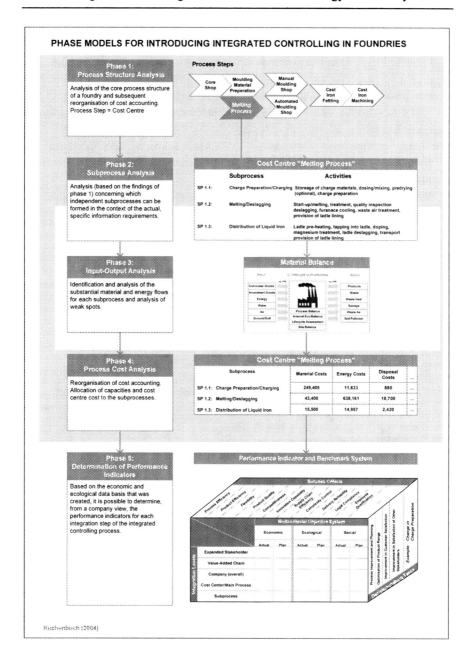

Fig. 5.3. Phase model for introducing integrated controlling in foundries[10]

---

[10] Source: Kuchenbuch 2004; also see Lange and Kuchenbuch 2003, p. 32

5.2.1 Phase 0: Information Requirements Analysis

The starting point for the information requirements analysis is "stakeholder scanning"[11], a tool system for identifying the interests of potentially strategically relevant interaction partners on a company, co-operation and/ or (expanded) stakeholder level. It comprises identifying and characterising the potential market and non-market related stakeholder groups as well as the analysis, forecasting and evaluation of the interests and expectations concerning the achievement of objectives on the part of these stakeholders with regards to the company.

In the project conducted, the following stakeholder groups were identified as being particularly relevant in terms of strategic factors:[12]

Table 5.2. Stakeholders of strategic relevance for foundries

	Stakeholders	Potential Interests/ Requirements
Internal	Management	• Power, influence, prestige (regarding ecological aspects as well) • Development/ realisation of own ideas/ capabilities
	Employees	• Income (workplace/ job) • Environment-oriented workplace • Ecological image of company • Social security and contacts
	Shareholders	• Preservation of invested capital; return and appreciation on invested capital • Inclusion of environmental aspects in due diligence reviews • Opportunities for participation

---

[11] See Horváth 2003, p. 401 et seq. and the literature references provided there
[12] See Dyllick 1984, p. 75; Lange et al. 2001, pp. 52-88; Pohl 2001, pp. 59-63

Table 5.2. (Cont.)

	Stakeholders	Potential Interests/Requirements
External	Residents	• As a rule, directly affected by noise and odour emissions.
	Authorities	• Supervisory body for compliance with immission limits and regulations related to environmental protection • Commissioning of regulated equipment, plants and facilities subject to approval • Inspection of MAK (maximum concentrations at the workplace) values.
	Customers	• Automobile manufacturers make a variety of demands with respect to the ecological composition and impact of products • Inclusion of ecological factors in the criteria for selecting suppliers
	Banks	• Consideration of ecological risks when granting loans • Possible damage to bank's image if a customer appears or is perceived as being harmful to the environment • Inclusion of environmental factors when conducting ratings
	Insurance Companies	• Consideration of ecological risks in the course of incident analyses • More favourable conditions in regards to employer's liability insurance (product risk) and the German environmental liability law (facility liability) for companies with active environmental protection policies/ environmental protection management

Based on the requirements of the relevant stakeholders and the company objectives derived from them, the analysis of the significant economic, ecological and social decision-making tasks to be met by the management of a foundry, as well as the information requirements associated with them, forms the starting point of Phase 0. Therefore, it is important to expressly point out here that the definition of decision-making tasks is explicitly not under the responsibility of Controlling, but rather incumbent on the company management.

5.2.2 Phase 1: Process Structure Analysis

The goal of the process structure analysis is to identify a company's value-adding business processes. This analysis creates the organisational basis for determining the material and energy flows, for reorganising the costing and thus for integrating information relevant to decision-making onto identical reference objects. In the first phase of the INPROCESS PROJECT, the process structures of the participating foundries were recorded and documented and the value-adding core processes of a foundry were identified by way of derivation. While the individual subprocesses can vary depending on the product spectrum and product process, the following seven process steps can be considered as pivotal to the net product of sand foundries.[13]

- Core Shop
- Moulding Material Preparation
- Manual Moulding Shop
- Automated Moulding Shop
- Melting Process
- Cast Iron Fettling
- Cast Iron Machining

From a costing viewpoint, the identified process structures described above represent the minimum manifestation of the main processes to be generated. Whether or not additional cost centres or sub-cost centres (for the direct production area) have to be set up depends on the respective information requirements. Thus, e.g., it is conceivable that the "melting process" process step can be further subdivided into "charge preparation" and "melting plant" process step. This would then be practical if, within the melting process, a large number of melting units are bundled, which also vary in their dimensions and melt various liquid iron qualities. In this case, the integration into one single cost centre would result in a loss of information due to the aggregation. The number of cost centres to be formed is thus dependent on the respective internal/ operational context.

In view of the decision-making orientation underlying the integrated controlling method, however, it is important that the cost centre structure be aligned along the internal value-added chain, to ensure that the integration of material, energy and cost-based data onto identical reference objects is subsequently successful.[14]

5.2.3 Phase 2: Subprocess Analysis

Based on the results of the process structure analysis, the subprocesses then have to be identified for each defined process step within each respective cost centre, using an iterative reconciliation process between material and energy flow accounting and process-oriented costing. It must

---

[13] Due it its relative independence and low material and energy expenditure, the model making shop is not taken into consideration here.
[14] See Kuchenbuch et al. 2003, p. 36; Lange and Kuchenbuch 2003, p. 30

be ensured that only those subprocesses are defined for which both an activity-based cost allocation and a determination of the material and energy flows can be carried out based on economic factors.

The procedure: first, the tasks carried out within a cost centre are determined. In a second step, the individual tasks are condensed into homogeneous "task bundles", which are called subprocesses in the following. These subprocesses represent the integration level or reference objects for which both the material and energy flows as well as the cost information have to be determined.

5.2.4 Phase 3: Input-Output Analysis

The central point of the material and energy flow accounting is the preparation of a complete and consistent input-output analysis. Taking into account the production-specific relationships between resource utilisation, products, waste and emissions, all the inputs and outputs needed for covering the information requirements are determined for the defined subprocesses. To this end, the available data on all company levels first has to be collected and a systematic analysis then conducted to verify completeness and consistency. Any missing data has to be supplemented by means of measurements, calculations or assumptions.[15] The following chart illustrates a checklist indicating the essential areas for which data has to be collected on the subprocess level of a foundry.

---

[15] See Kuchenbuch et al. 2003, p. 36

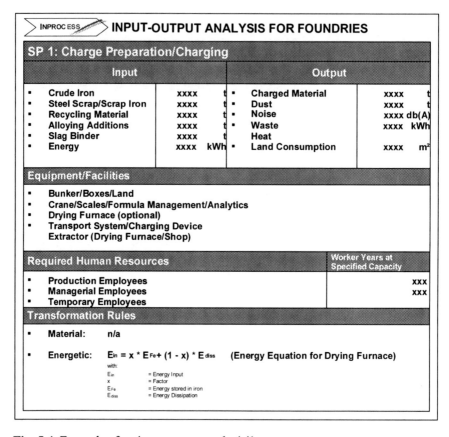

Fig. 5.4. Example of an input-output analysis[16]

The data that has thus been determined and checked for consistency can be visualised in a Sankey Diagram. The following diagram provides an example of the possible material flow of a melting process:

---

[16] Source: Kuchenbuch et al. 2003, p. 36

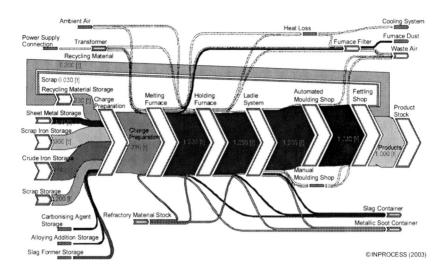

Fig. 5.5. Sankey diagram of the material flows for the melting operation core process.[17]

As the Sankey Diagram shows, the moulding shop and cast iron machining/ fettling shop are core processes which should be allowed for in the analysis of the melting process, since they serve to assist in the integrated analysis of the material flows (recycling material and scrap) (Rebhan 1999; Rebhan 2000). To obtain indicators about weak spots and optimisation potentials, it is practical to derive indices from this data that can be used for internal and external benchmarking. Once the starting points for the optimisation measures have been identified, their technical and organisational feasibility has to be analysed. The effects of these measures on the material and energy flows within the company, and – in conjunction with the corresponding broadening of the focus of the examination – on a cross-company basis as well, can subsequently be determined along the entire value-added chain. Utilising the MEAS-System[18] in the foundries participating in the INPROCESS project, the project team succeeded in compiling a series of starting points for optimisation measures. Furthermore, prior to actually implementing the measures, deployment of the AUDIT software simulated the effects on the material and energy flows as well as the costs associated with them.

---

[17] Reference quantity: one ton of machine moulded sound castings (Source: Kuchenbuch et al. 2003, p. 37)

[18] Meas = Material and Energy Analysis System.

5.2.5 Phase 4: Process Cost Analysis

Concept of Environmental Activity-based Costing

Described in the following, the approach of a process-oriented environmental activity-based costing method for the foundry industry is conceptually based on the basic idea of activity-based costing (formulated in the USA).[19] Activity-based costing is a process-oriented costing system that focuses on a transparent and (to the greatest extent possible) activity-based cost allocation for the direct performance areas of a company. Within the scope of the INPROCESS project, this system was further developed with respect to environmental aspects. The central point is the integration of material and energy data with cost-oriented information to identical objects under consideration. To this end, the subprocesses of each cost centre, which function as integration levels, have to be defined in close co-ordination with the material and energy flow accounting.

The approach is distinguished by the following characteristics:

- Process orientation in cost centre and cost unit accounting
- Usage of cost concept(s) augmented by environmental aspects
- Differentiated identification of costs relevant to decision-making and the environment as well as the essential material and energy flows of each subprocess[20]
- Focus on the direct production areas
- Separate (informal) identification of the recycling material costs for each subprocess
- Extensive use of reference quantities from the material and energy flow accounting
- Conceptualised as parallel accounting
- Documentation/ recording of environmental impact solely in the form of internalised costs and completely documented material and energy flows, i.e. no analysis of external effects.

As has already been described in detail in the process-structure analysis section, it is necessary to create cost centres along the internal value-added chain of a foundry, as that is the only way to ensure that the material and energy data as well as the process-oriented cost data are allocated to identical reference objects and thus guarantee a consistent data basis for the

---

[19] See Miller and Vollmann 1985; Pfohl and Stölzle 1991; Coenenberg 2003, pp. 205-230; Horváth 2003, 543 et seq.; Schweitzer and Küpper 2003, pp. 345-381
[20] For more on the differentiated identification of material and energy flows, see Kuchenbuch et al. 2003.

performance indicator-supported provision of information via integrated controlling. The precise implementation of the environmental activity-based costing approach will be explained in more depth in the following sections.

Cost Element Accounting

Due to its concept as a parallel accounting method, environmental activity-based costing is based on the existing cost element structure of conventional costing accounting. Since not all cost elements[21] for a foundry – in terms of both economic and ecological aspects – carry the same importance, the cost elements should be aggregated into basic cost element groups. In addition to condensing the information, the advantage of such a process is that it also reduces complexity, which is important for the acceptance of the costing method. On the basis of the concept of environmental costs[22] and the information requirements of integrated controlling, we recommend creating the following cost element groups and disclosing them in both the cost centre accounting (per subprocess) and the cost unit accounting (per product):

- Material Costs
- Energy Costs
- Personnel Costs
- Internal Performance
- Calculatory Capital Costs

- Maintenance Costs
- Waste Disposal Costs
- Allocation 1: General
- Allocation 2: Administration and Sales
- Allocation 3: Production Support

Furthermore, a review should be conducted, taking into account the specific internal decision-making situation and information requirements, to determine whether it is necessary to differentiate each cost element group according to conventional and environmentally relevant costs.

Cost Centre Accounting

The structural design of the cost centre accounting is based on the results of the subprocess analysis.[23] Here, the subprocesses for which process-oriented cost data now has to be ascertained were determined for each cost centre. Against this background, the cost centre costs, which can be taken from the conventional costing and distributed according to the cost ele-

---

[21] See DGV 1996, pp. 23-26
[22] For more on the concept of environmental costs, see Lange and Kuchenbuch 2003a, p. 24 et seq.
[23] See Kuchenbuch et al. 2003, p. 36 et seq.

ment groups described above, have to be allocated to the defined sub-processes. For this, the process cost analysis should include a check to determine, for each cost element, how to allocate them to the subprocesses. It should be noted here that the effort involved in collecting data for the allocation key is justifiably proportionate to the required accuracy. The determination of possible allocation keys is elaborated on in the following, using the example of the *Energy Cost* element:

Basically, energy costs can then be best allocated if the consumption volume of each consuming unit is recorded via a counter or meter. From a costing viewpoint, such an allocation key would be the most suitable and thus is assigned priority 1. However, in practice, this process approach leads to insignificant difficulties. It is associated with considerable expense, since each unit has to be equipped with a meter/ counter; moreover, it has to be ensured that the meter/ counter readings are read for each reporting or accounting period and forwarded to the Costing. Furthermore the installation of meters/ counters for large units is practical and feasible, while a separate meter/ counter for the lighting of a cost centre hardly seems realisable in terms of practical considerations. If continuous consumption measurements are not possible or practical, the next option is to rely on reference and target values (priority 2). These values can be determined on the basis on the technical consumption data. Thus, e.g,. for a holding furnace, such a target value can be determined by means of the installed capacity and the elapsed operating hours. The third option to be considered is a proportional distribution based on empirical values (priority 3). This process usually leads to quick results, but is characterised by a very high degree of inaccuracy and subjectivity. As a starting point for a more precise analysis, however, it does appear quite suitable.

In the practical implementation of this approach, therefore, a mix of the respective data collection options should always be employed. It is thus expected that particularly important equipment (e.g. a melting furnace) is equipped with a meter/ counter for internal monitoring purposes, whereas other units (e.g. suction apparatuses) are controlled via reference and target values or via proportional allocation based on empirical values (e.g. hall lighting). In regards to the operational dependency of the costs and the issue of reduction associated with it, the variable and fixed cost elements have to be determined, as far as possible, for each cost element group. This information is important in terms of decision-making situations, e.g. in connection with break-even analyses, and provides information about the temporal reduction of the costs. To ensure a realistic evaluation of the both the recycling material and the scrap quantity, a separate recognition and cost-related evaluation should be carried out along the lines of flow cost accounting.[24] To this end, the total costs of each subprocess – different-

---

[24] See Gay 1998; LfU (Landesamt für Umweltschutz/ State Environmental Protection Agency) 1999; Strobel and Wagner 1999

tiated according to the aforementioned cost element groups – have to be allocated to the "sound castings" as well as the recycling material and scrap. An allocation is carried out in dependence on the reference quantity, via which the process costs are also allocated to the products.

Cost Unit Accounting

Within the scope of the cost unit accounting, it must then be determined as to which product will utilise what process (main process or subprocess) and to what extent. To this end, depending on the desired accuracy level, there is the option of allocating the costs originated by the subprocesses via a common reference quantity per cost centre or a reference quantity per subprocess. Here as well, it must be noted that with a rising number of reference quantities, the effort involved in collecting the data also increases and the complexity mounts. By way of illustration, it should be assumed that the process costs of the melting process cost centre example are allocated to the cost units via the standardised *product weight* reference quantity. In a first step, the determination must be made with respect to what extent an individual product has utilised the reference quantity. For this, the specific weight of an individual product is multiplied with its output during the period and then this sum is compared in proportion to the total weight of all products. The thus determined percentage or equivalent figure is then used for allocating the subprocess costs to the products. In a second step, the subprocess costs for each product are calculated by multiplying the subprocess costs with this equivalent figure; a subsequent division by the output of this product determines the unit costs.

5.2.6 Phase 5: Performance Indicator-supported Provision of Information

Consistent and systematic implementation of the first four phases (process structure, subprocess, input/ output and process costs analyses) of the model for introducing integrated controlling into foundries creates a data basis which, from a company or corporate standpoint, enables a far-reaching *complete* provision of information for the respective stake-holders.[25] Based on this data, a performance indicator model is created in Phase 5, which is intended to assist the management of a foundry in making objective-oriented decisions in terms of controlling, particularly in

---

[25] See Lange and Kuchenbuch 2003, p. 30 et seq.

order to exploit potentials for saving costs and resources.[26] In light of the respective information requirements as well as the expansion stages of integrated controlling, a performance indicator system is needed that ensures the provision of information pertaining to all relevant stakeholders. However, it must be taken into consideration that not only those performance indicators that can be derived from the material, energy and cost-oriented data should be used. Furthermore, the main task is to broaden the scope of consideration as well as map such information in the form of performance indicators, which – in the sense of DIN 14031 – can generally be termed environmental management and environmental condition indicators.[27] When developing this model, the objective is thus to create a flexible system based on the data basis; a system which, depending on the information requirements of the management, can provide data relevant to decision-making in the form of performance indicators. For this reason, a rigid system is not presented in the following, but rather an open system that ensures the flexible provision of information. Based on these general conditions, the following performance indicator systematic is recommended:

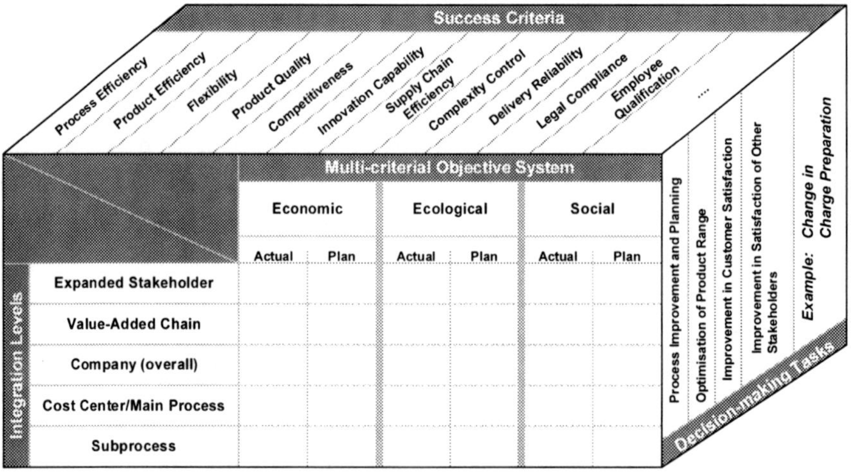

Fig. 5.6. Multidimensional performance indicator model of integrated controlling[28]

---

[26] See Lange et al. 2003, p. 32

[27] See Lange et al 2003a, pp. 217-221

[28] Source: Author. For more on this content, see Kuchenbuch et al. 2004, p. 27. Note: The "Decision-making Tasks" dimension contains a column titled 'Example: Changes in Charge Preparation Accounting'. This refers to an example used in Chapter 3 for the purpose of documenting the process sequence along the phase model.

The first starting point for creating and implementing the performance indicator model described above is to derive the most important decisions that have to be made by the management of a foundry. However, a mere analysis of the relevant decision-making tasks is usually not sufficient for determining specific indicators. Therefore, the essential success/ performance criteria have to be defined for each decision-making task. Table 5.12 (in Section 5.3.2) lists examples of possible success criteria for each of the three dimensions of sustainability (economy, ecology, social). Nevertheless, the question of what success criterion is significant for which decision-making task cannot be answered in general terms, but rather only in consideration of the specific company background. One or more indicators have to be determined for the operationalisation of each of these success criteria

By utilising the underlying process structure, the performance indicators can be generated on all levels of the process model (e.g. subprocess, main process, cost centre and company levels) and consolidated via the respective material-energy transformation[29] and/ or organisational aggregation rules. Other levels of consideration include the *value-added chain* and *expanded stakeholder levels* derived from the integration steps of integrated controlling.

The objective of using the performance indicators is to enable the evaluation of alternative system statuses. A comparison of system statuses can take the form of a period comparison, actual/target comparison or a system comparison conducted prior and subsequent to implementing technical-organisational measures. To this end, in the performance indicator system outlined here, ecological and, if applicable, social indicators are used in addition to the classical economic indicators (Reichmann 2001, pp. 51-112), thus creating the pre-requisite for sustainable company management (Kuchenbuch et al. 2004, p. 28). The generated indicators represent measuring points or sensors in companies that enable the documentation of changes and the provision of information regarding the reasons for the changes. A more detailed example of this is presented in Section 5.3.6.

---

[29] In the context of material flow accounting, 'transformation rules' are to be seen as the rules for calculating a specific output structure (horizontal data compression) from a given input structure and the associated data (e.g. originating from a system in a plant). In contrast, 'aggregation' refers to a vertical compression of data across various organisational levels.

5.3 Case Study: Model Foundry

The model foundry was developed within the scope of the BMBF INPROCESS project with the intention of evaluating the project results for the focuses of the integrated controlling project, the process-oriented environmental activity-based costing as well as the material and energy flow accounting. The goal was to find a foundry layout that depicted all the significant findings of the case studies[30] conducted in the INPROCESS project. Moreover, the model foundry served as an illustrative example for the industry guidelines. By way of these guidelines, the results of the project were distributed to the industry via German Foundry Association.

The structures, material and energy flows[31], as well as the costs associated therein, that are documented in the following represent the attempt to depict the complexity and heterogeneity of the approx. 250 foundries in the Federal Republic of Germany in one model. The project team was consequently faced with the challenge of generalising the various process variant options, particularly in regards to the melting units, moulding processes, company sizes, casting qualities, etc., and integrating them into the model in a way that would enable the description of a as large as possible part of the actually existing foundries.

According to both the INPROCESS team and the participating experts from the foundries, both the cost data described as well as the material and energy flows depict a realistic representation of the production structures and the production range. However, it should be pointed out here that a model must always inevitably be a simplified version of the real thing.

---

[30] In the project, a total of nine case studies were conducted in the participating foundries, with different thematic focuses. On the one hand, the respective focuses were selected because they were more relevant to the respective company, and on the other, the selection ensured that all essential issues relevant to the research project were addressed. This allowed the project team to work out solution approaches for specific questions and make these findings available to the other foundries in a general form within the framework of the model foundry.

[31] Here, we would like to thank all the employees of the participating project partners (Institut für Gießereitechnik, Düsseldorf/Germany; Aröw – Gesellschaft für Arbeits-, Reorganisations- und Ökologische Wirtschaftsberatung mbH, Duisburg/Germany) for their work and contribution.

5.3.1 Basic Structure of the Model Foundry

The Guss GmbH foundry is integrated into a mechanical engineering company as a 100% subsidiary. The company is an internal supplier of compressor pumps, which it manufactures in five production series. The product spectrum comprises small heating water pumps up to large feed pumps for waste water, sludge and oil. The largest piece of equipment produced is a turbo-compressor weighing approx. eleven tons. Each of these pumps consists of an upper and lower section, suction flange, motor flange as well as an impeller. Thus, the production range includes a total of 25 casting parts, which, depending on the part to be manufactured, are produced in two casting qualities (grey and spheroidal graphite cast iron).[32] The casting parts are mechanically machined and varnished by the company's in-house departments. i.e. in the mechanical engineering department. Guss GmbH is internally divided into the following departments:

- Management/ Administration
- Purchasing, Engineering and Design, Sales, Shipping, Plant Security and Safety
- Melting Shop (incl. delivery, charge preparation, treatment and processing, ladle system)
- Manual moulding shop with two mixers for furan resin-bonded sand
- Automated moulding shop (incl. bentonite-bonded sand and coldbox cores)
- Fettling Shop (incl. manual fettling stations, blasting chamber and overhead conveyor blasting unit)
- Core Shop
- Sand Treatment (incl. mixer and mechanical sand regeneration)
- Annealing Bay
- Maintenance
- Models are procured from a specialised supplier.

In the following, based on the information presented this far, the results of the process analysis will first be documented and then the recording of the respective material and energy flows as well as the corresponding cost data for each process will be described.

---

[32] This paper refrains from documenting the respective product formulas and process-related transformation rules; please refer to the final project report. See INPROCESS Final Report, Deutscher Gießereiverband (German Foundry Association) 2004.

5.3.2 Phase 0: Information Requirement Analysis

The departure point for the considerations is the decision-making tasks derived from the respective company objectives as well as the associated information requirements on the part of the management of a foundry. In this context, the following tasks play a particularly important role:

- process improvement and process planning,
- optimisation of product range,
- improvement in customer satisfaction, and
- improvement in the satisfaction of other stakeholders.

In order to be able to manage these tasks, the most significant, foundry-specific economic, ecological and social performance/ success criteria were elaborated in the course of the project; the criteria varied in their degree of importance, depending on the respective decision-making task. These criteria are described in the following table:

Table 5.3. Selected economic, ecological and social performance/ success criteria in foundries[33]

Economic Dimension	Ecological Dimension	Social Dimension
• Econ. Process Efficiency • Econ. Product Efficiency • Flexibility • Product Quality • Competitiveness • Innovation Capability • Efficiency of Supply Chain Management • Customer Relationship Management • Complexity Control • Delivery Reliability • Minimisation of Liability Risk	• Ecolog. Process Efficiency • Ecolog. Product Efficiency • Legal Compliance	• Company/ Corporate Image at the Location • Assurance of Workplaces • Occupational and Health Safety • Employee Qualification

In order to be able to illustrate the individual phases and tools by way of a homogeneous example, it is necessary to reduce the complexity. Based on the current trends on the raw materials markets, the following decision-making situations for the management of a foundry are assumed:

---

[33] Source: Kuchenbuch et al. 2004; VDG 2001, p. 40

Example: In 2004, the booming economic development, especially in China, caused a raw material shortage in the steel scrap sector. China's steel imports had increased by approx. 50% in the previous year, resulting in a corresponding doubling of the steel prices[34]. The resultant demand on the world market also led to a considerably lower supply of steel scrap in Europe and Germany, along with a higher market price associated with it. In view of these developments, many foundries are now faced with the question of how to respond to the steel scrap shortage. Accordingly, an examination should be conducted with respect to the possibility of how to substitute the steel scrap charge material with cast iron scrap without resulting in quality changes. To this end, the question of what effects such a change in the charge preparation will have and what indicators should be applied for the controlling needs to be addressed. The primary focus is thus to demonstrate how the integrated controlling tool can be utilised to provide the necessary data. This creates the prerequisite of transparently presenting the effects associated with the substitution process.

5.3.3 Phase 1: Process Structure Analysis

Based on the findings of Phase 0, the current organisational structure was documented as well as analysed and optimised within the scope of the process structure and subprocess analyses. The focus of attention here was particularly on the direct production area, i.e., to put it conversely, the administration and sales cost centres were not examined. The reason for this was first and foremost due to the fact that in the underlying research project, the significant material and energy flows as well as the development of a process-oriented environmental activity-based costing method were the subjects under examination.

As already shown in 5.2.2, at least seven value-adding core processes could be identified on the basis of the case studies conducted and the expert knowledge of the German Foundry Association and the German Institute of Foundry Technology. In regards to the cost accounting, this constitutes a minimum categorisation of the cost centres. Diverging from this categorisation, the following cost centres were created for the specific application case of the model foundry:

- CC 1: Melting Process
- CC 2: Manual Moulding Shop
- CC 3: Sand Regeneration
- CC 4: Automated Moulding Shop
- CC 5: Sand Treatment
- CC 6: Core Shop
- CC 7: Blasting Chamber
- CC 8: Blasting System
- CC 9: Fettling Shop
- CC 10: Annealing Bay

---

[34] See www.weyland.at/index.php?id=198, version dated 07-06-2004.

5.3.4 Phase 2: Subprocess Analysis

After conducting the process structure analysis, the essential subprocesses within each of the model foundry's cost centres were identified. At this point, the previously conducted task analysis will not be described further.

The goal of the subprocess analysis is to combine all the tasks carried out within a cost centre into homogeneous bundles, called the "subprocesses". Furthermore, here, the suppositions should already be taken into account in regards to how the subprocesses can be combined into main processes within the scope of the environmental activity-based costing. The resultant structures then form the basis for the cost allocation to the reference objects. The following table provides an overview of the results of the subprocess analysis conducted for the model foundry.

Table 5.4. Subprocess analysis and main process allocation[35]

CC	SP No.	Subprocess Name	MP Allocation
CC 1 Melting Process	1.1	Charge Preparation/ Charging	1
	1.2	Melting/ Deslagging	1
	1.3	Distribution of Liquid Iron	1
CC 2 Manual Moulding Shop	2.1	Mould Making	2
	2.2	Mould Casting	70 % = 1 30 % = 2
	2.3	Cooling of Casting	2
CC 3 Sand Regeneration	3.1	Unpacking	3
	3.2	Sand Regeneration	3
CC 4 Automated Moulding Shop	4.1	Mould Making/ Pouring	4
	4.2	Cooling of Casting	4
	4.3	Unpacking	4
CC 5 Sand Treatment	5.1	Used Sand Treatment	5
	5.2	Treatment of Moulding Material	5
CC 6 Core Shop	6.1	Treatment of Moulding Material	6
	6.2	Core Making	6
	6.3	Finishing/ Drying	6

[35] Source: Kuchenbuch 2004

Table 5.4. (Cont.)

CC 7 Blasting Chamber		7.1	Blasting	7
		7.2	Treatment of Blasting Agent	7
CC 8 Blasting System		8.1	Blasting	7
		8.2	Treatment of Blasting Agent	7
CC 9 Fettling Shop		9.1	Handling of Recycling Materials	8
		9.2	Fettling MC	8
		9.3	Fettling ML	8
CC 10 Annealing Bay		10.1	Furnace Charging	9
		10.2	Annealing	9
		10.3	Quench Hardening	9

The results of the subprocess analysis from table 5.4 are displayed in the following diagram, so that the production-technical and organisational interconnections are roughly mapped. The precise analysis of the technical-organisational and particularly the material and energy flow interlinkings are topics for the following 'Phase 3: Input-Output Analysis'.

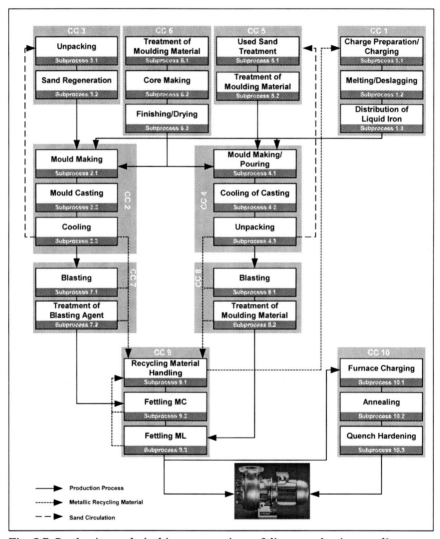

Fig. 5.7. Production-technical interconnections of direct production area[36]

---

[36] Source: Kuchenbuch 2004

5.3.5 Phase 3: Input-Output Analysis

In the input-output analysis, the material-energetic changes triggered by the respective decision-making tasks are registered. As already discussed, this analysis utilises the described process model and includes the determination of all material-energetic and technical-organisational transformation rules. On this basis, the actual data for 2004 was collected and the planning for 2005 was carried out for the model foundry. The results are summarised in table 5.5.

Note: Due to the number of processes, only the subprocesses of 'Cost Centre 1: Melting Process' (see Table 5.4) are examined in the following, since the significant material-energetic changes become apparent here due to the nature of the example.

Since the described transformation rules are taken as a basis for these figures, the resultant changes can be both traced backed to their causal factors and analysed in Controlling:

- The planned substitution process definitely leads to an increase in the quantity of the utilised materials (cast iron scrap and steel scrap). The reason for this is that in the 2005 plan, more material has to be used to provide the identical volume of liquid iron, since the proportion of slag in the charge preparation material increases. This is attributed to the higher degree of pollution (i.e. lower level of purity) in the cast iron scrap.
- The changes in the melting energy consumption have to be analysed against the background of the following opposite developments: since less energy is required for melting cast iron scrap, an increase in usage inevitably leads to a reduction of the melting energy. However, since more input material (skelp iron) has to be melted in order to provide the same volume of liquid iron, the energy usage is thus increased. On the whole, a constant, absolute energy consumption is therefore assumed in the example.
- Since cast iron scrap is generally more similar in substance to the required final alloy of the liquid iron, less alloying and aggregate materials are needed in terms of process materials.
- The increased slag generated by the higher degree of pollution of the cast iron scrap and the effects described above also lead to an increase of metallic soot in the furnace (metallic adherences on the furnace lining, especially in the furnace edge area). The direct effect of this is a rise in the number of furnace lining replacements, which is associated with increased consumption of refractory materials in the melting furnace and increases the corresponding waste item on the output side.

- In this context, an increase in the "Furnace Dust" output item can also be seen. Incineration of the adherences produces more dust in the waste air, which is then filtered out and has to be disposed of as waste. The higher demand on the filter performance increases the dust particle emissions, which are diffused into the environment.

Table 5.5. Input-output analysis: example[37]

	SP No.	Input		Actual 2004	Planned 2005
Material	1.1	Cast Iron Scrap	t	5,304.40	6,594.57
	1.1	Steel Scrap	t	6,199.47	5,000.00
	1.1	Recycling Material	t	1,943.75	1943.75
	1.1	Scrap	t	825.58	825.58
Process Materials	1.1	Carburising Agents	t	206.17	165.00
	1.1	Ferrosilicon	t	105.25	85.00
	1.2	Refractory Material	t	28.77	29.50
	1.3	Refractory Material	t	4.33	4.33
Energy	1.2	Melting Energy	kWh	7,770,959.00	7,770,959.00
	1.2	Ventilation Energy	kWh	67,600.17	67,600.17
	1.2	Gas (Ladle Furnace)	kWh	193,143.35	193,143.35
Other	1.2	Supply Air	Nm³	46,875,000.00	46,875,000.00

	SP No.	Output		Actual 2004	Planned 2005
Input Material	1.3	Liquid Iron	t	14,416.57	14,416.57
	1.3	Liquid Iron Energy	kWh	5,154,207.00	5.154.207.00
Waste	1.2	Slag	t	162.92	170.50
	1.2	Refractory Material	t	10.09	10.82
	1.2	Metallic Soot in Furnace	t	18.75	19.25
	1.2	Furnace Dust	t	4.33	4.65
	1.3	Slag	t	2.88	2.93
	1.3	Refractory Material	t	1.44	1.44

---

[37] Source: Kuchenbuch 2004. The quantity specifications refer to an annual production output of 11,648.04 tons. Also see Footnote 116.

Table 5.5. (Cont.)

	1.2	Waste Heat	kWh	2,370,096.26	2,370,096.26
Other	1.2	Dust Emissions	kg	375.00	515.63
	1.2	Waste Air	Nm³	46,875,000.00	46,875,000.00
	1.3	Waste Heat	kWh	507,399.26	507,399.26

5.3.6 Phase 4: Process Cost Analysis

On the basis of the quantity specifications, the respective primary process costs can be calculated for all material and energy flows that are procured by the company on the input side or which have to be disposed of at the company's expense on the output side (also refer to Table 5.6). In addition to the costs arising from the respective input and output quantities, further direct process costs and indirect process costs are shown on a subprocess level within the scope of the environmental activity-based costing. Further direct process costs include, e.g., personnel costs, maintenance expenses and calculatory or imputed costs. Moreover, not all cost centre costs can be allocated – particularly in regards to economic aspects. Thus, there is always a certain portion of costs that has to be allocated to the subprocesses as indirect process costs.[38] They then have to be consolidated into the respective main processes and from there, further allocated to the products. In the model foundry, for the purpose of reducing complexity, only 9 main processes were worked with, which were largely oriented on the cost centre structure. Table 5.4 shows what subprocesses were allocated to which main process. The following diagram illustrates the main processes of the model foundry.

---

[38] For more in-depth information on the topic of allocating cost centre costs to the subprocesses, see Lange and Kuchenbuch (2003a); Kuchenbuch 2004

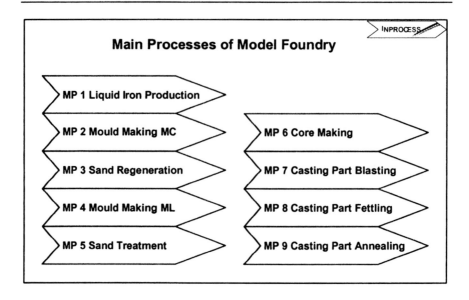

Fig. 5.8. Main processes of model foundry[39]

Figure 5.9 provides an overview of the total costs of various reference objects.[40] It also contains an aggregated form of the primary costs from table 5.6.[41]

---

[39] MC = Manual Casting; ML = Moulding Line (Source: Kuchenbuch et al. 2003, p. 34)

[40] The exact way in which these costs are calculated in environmental activity-based costing is documented in detail in Lange and Kuchenbuch 2003a

[41] As already explained, Table 5.6 contains only the cost data for the spheroidal graphite cast iron, while the costs pertaining to Subprocess 1.1. and Main Process 1 are calculated as a sum total arising from spheroidal graphite and grey cast iron. A more in-depth examination would not provide provide higher informational value, but rather only have an adverse impact on the clarity. The specific alloy was only taken into account in the product analysis.

Table 5.6. Direct process costs: example[42]

	SP No.	Input		Actual 2004	Planned 2005
Material	1.1	Cast Iron Scrap	€	689,572.00	1,384,859.70
	1.1	Steel Scrap	€	805,931.10	1,000,000.00
	1.1	Recycling Material	€		
	1.1	Scrap	€		
Process Materials	1.1	Carburising Agents	€	98,960.64	79,200.00
	1.1	Ferrosilicon	€	73,672.90	59,500.00
	1.2	Refractory Material	€	17,262.00	17,700.00
	1.3	Refractory Material	€	2,598.00	2,598.00
Energy	1.2	Melting Energy	€	466,257.54	466,257.54
	1.2	Ventilation Energy	€	4,056.01	4,056,.01
	1.2	Gas (Ladle Furnace)	€	5,214.87	5,214.87
	SP No.	Output		Actual 2004	Planned 2005
Input Material	1.3	Liquid Iron	€		
	1.3	Liquid Iron Energy	€		
Waste	1.2	Slag	€	8,960.60	9,377.50
	1.2	Waste: Refractory Material	€	554.95	595.10
	1.2	Metallic Soot in Furnace	€	1,031.25	1,058.75
	1.2	Furnace Dust	€	389.25	418.50
	1.3	Slag	€	158.42	161.15
	1.3	Waste: Refractory Material	€	79.21	79.20

---

[42] Source: Kuchenbuch 2004. The quantity specifications refer to an annual production output of 11,648.04 tons of spheroidal graphite cast iron and therefore do not include the costs for the grey cast iron. Instead of cast iron scrap, crude iron is used for the production of grey cast iron, thus the decision-making situation applied in the example only impacts the spheroidal graphite cast iron.

Note: A change in the indirect process costs is not assumed in the example. The supposition that the calculatory and imputed costs for both periods under observation are assumed identical has to be understood from this standpoint. Changes apply to the costs for analysing the alloys as well as for the rise in the number of furnace lining replacements and the associated increase in the corresponding disposal item. These additional costs – as seen in Figure 5.9. – were accounted for in the 'Maintenance', 'Production Support' and ' Disposal Costs' cost unit groups in the 2005 planning. Furthermore, rising prices for both cast iron scrap (from 130 to 210 €/t) and steel scrap (from 130 to 200 €/t) have also been allowed for in the cost accounting.

The allocation interrelationships within the scope of the environmental activity-based costing will be illustrated by means of the reference objects presented in Figure 5.9. As previously explained, the subproccesses represent the central reference object for the integrated controlling method. This is the basis for consolidating both the material-energetic and cost-oriented data. As is shown in table 5.4, Subprocess 1.1 is allocated to Main Process (MP) 1: 'Liquid Iron Production' on a 100 percent basis. This MP is a cost collector for Subprocess (SP) 1.2 and 1.3 (each on a hundred percent basis) as well as SP 2.2 (at seventy percent). From here, the costs are further allocated depending on the extent to which a product utilises a main process. The costs of MP 1 are calculated to the respective products via the 'Required Iron Quantity' cost driver. A total of approx. 426,430.90 kg[43] of liquid iron are needed to produce the 'Type D Impeller' product, which corresponds to a proportional share of approx. 2.29%[44] of the entire liquid iron volume. With the aid of this equivalent figure, the costs of the main process are then passed on to the product. To calculate the unit cost, the specified total product cost has to be divided by 2000 (The difference in the production quantity is explained by the scrapping of 105 units).

---

[43] Calculation: production quantity 2,105 units; 202.58 kg/unit; total volume of liquid iron: 18,620,350 kg.

[44] For the calculation, the exact values in Figure 5.9. were calculated to all decimal places.

Reference Objects / Costs	Subprocess 1.1		Main Process 1		Typ D: Impeller	
	Actual 2004	Plan 2005	Actual 2004	Plan 2005	Actual 2004	Plan 2005
Direct Process Costs						
Direct Material Costs	2,018,079.00	3,072,813.20	2,018,079.00	3,072,813.20	66,280.15	82,340.46
Material Costs	249,405.00	215,472.00	275,102.00	241,607.00	6,300.20	5,533.12
Energy Costs	00.00	00.00	621,495.00	621,495.00	14,233.07	14,233.07
Personnel Costs	80,200.00	80,200.00	487,277.10	487,277.10	11,159.30	11,159.30
Internal Services Costs	15,700.00	15,700.00	48,225.00	48,225.00	1,104.42	1,104.42
Calc. Costs	18,000.00	18,000.00	242,787.50	242,787.50	5,560.17	5,560.17
Maintenance Costs	21,600.00	21,600.00	277,275.00	280,515.00	6,349.97	6,424.17
Disposal Costs	00.00	00.00	16,719.00	17,235.53	382.89	394.72
Indirect Process Costs						
Material Costs	1,695.00	1,695.00	34,898.00	34,898.00	799.21	799.21
Energy Costs	11,633.00	11,633.00	45,111.00	45,111.00	1,033.10	1,033.10
Personnel Costs	00.00	00.00	00.00	00.00	00.00	00.00
Internal Services Costs	12,700.00	12,700.00	24,945.00	24,945.00	571.27	571.27
Calc. Costs	00.00	00.00	00.00	00.00	00.00	00.00
Maintenance Costs	00.00	00.00	00.00	00.00	00.00	00.00
Disposal Costs	880.00	880.00	5,281.00	5,809.10	120.94	133.04
Alloc. 1: General	28,880.00	22,880.00	385,517.50	385,517.50	8,828.87	8,828.87
Alloc. 2: Admin. + Sales	17,872.00	17,872.00	281,148.30	281,148.30	6,438.67	6,438.67
Alloc. 3: Prod. Support	3,900.00	3,900.00	27,969.10	29,669.10	640.53	679.46
Total	2,480,544.00	3,495,345.20	4,791,883.50	5,819,053.33	129,802.79	145,233.05

Main Process 1: Total from the costs of subprocesses 1.1, 1.2 and 1.3 as well 70% of the costs from SP 2.2

Typ D: Impeller: The costs are commensurate with 2.29% of the MP 1 costs. Product quantity: 2000 pieces CD: liquid iron volume

Fig. 5.9. Process costs of various reference objects (Source: Kuchenbuch 2004)

5.3.7 Phase 5: Performance Indicator-supported Provision of Information

As already discussed in Section 5.2.6, the main task of Phase 5 is the provision of stakeholder-oriented, performance indicator based information. As has been demonstrated, the focus lies more on the targeted supply of information pertaining to strategically relevant stakeholders with respect to a concrete decision-making situation and less on the development of a rigid performance indicator system with strictly defined contents.

But what indicators are necessary for supporting the decision-making situation described in the example and what indicators can be used to review the outcome of this decision?

First, material and energy oriented indicators should be defined for monitoring and controlling the resultant quantitative changes. Here, the focus is on those flows for which 'significant' quantitative changes have occurred (e.g. cast iron scrap, steel scrap, carburising agents, etc.) or on "sensitive" flows (e.g. dust emissions) that are very closely observed by certain stakeholders.

Examples of indicators to be developed: material usage and waste rates (kg per ton of sound castings; energy usage rates (kWh per ton of sound castings) and dust emissions (grams per standard cubic metre). In this context, particularly for materials and waste, individual performance indicators should be defined for the cast iron scrap, steel scrap, carburising agents, slag and furnace dust items.

Furthermore, in addition to a quantitative representation, there should also be a cost-related one. In the example under consideration, indicators that contain information about the resultant cost changes should especially be determined.

Examples of such indicators are: material usage and disposal cost coefficients (€ kWh per ton of sound castings).

For a thorough analysis of the effects of this decision, in addition to the indicators derived from the material and energy flow accounting as well as the environmental activity-based costing, such indicators should contain information that documents the technical-organisational changes. The most significant implications of the decision-making situation presented in the example are described in the following.

1. *Enhancement of Analytical Performance/ Quality Asssurance:* As a rule, increased use of cast iron scrap necessitates a greater number of chemical analyses of the alloy, in order to be able to guarantee the quality of the liquid iron. The less constant quality of the cast iron scrap can result in an insufficient alloy quality, which in turn can lead to increased scrap and waste in other production processes. For this reason,

the quality of the process for melting the required alloy has to be ensured through a preventive improvement in the analytical performance, or a possible error failure mode and effect analysis has to be conducted to check whether the resultant changes are tolerable[45]

Note: The following performance indicators should thus be determined: number of analyses per ton of sound castings; scrap/ waste rates (kg per ton of sound castings); number of subsequent alloyings per ton of sound castings.

2. *Filter Service Lives/ Emissions:* Since it generally has to be assumed that cast iron scrap contains more impurities than steel scrap (which also becomes manifest by the increase in the slag proportion), the melting furnace waste air is more severely polluted. As a result, more demand is placed on the filters, which reduces their service lives and may increase emissions (e.g. dust). Important indicators to be noted for these developments include: filter service lives in relation to the melting capacity per time interval; the filtered and to be disposed of dust quantity; dust emissions in the environment (g/Nm^3).

3. *Service Lives of Melting Furnaces:* Depending on the lumpiness as well as the weight of the cast iron scrap parts, a change in the wear and tear rate of the furnace lining can occur. It can generally be assumed that the increased use of cast iron scrap reduces the service life. As a result, the furnace has to be re-lined more often. However, for this process, the furnace has to be shut down, cooled off, re-lined and started up again. Since the furnace cannot be utilised for production, its efficiency decreases.

Note: In view of this, the following indicators should particularly be defined: furnace efficiency; melting capacity in tons per lining.

4. *Organisational Changes Concerning Charge Preparation:* Another issue that can arise in connection with the lumpiness of the cast iron scrap is the necessity of technical-organisational changes in the area of charge preparation (Subprocess 1.1). Depending on the condition of the cast iron scrap, large pieces may have to be crushed prior to use. Furthermore, the charge preparation process may take longer, since, due to the 'shapelessness' of the cast iron scrap, not as much material can be transported during each crane trip as is the case with, e.g., laminated sheet metal packs.

Note: Possible performance indicators here are: duration of the charge preparation process per furnace charging; space requirements of the material storage area; possible crushing time/ expense and effort in regards to the cast iron scrap.

---

[45] For more information about FMEA, see Ahsen and Lange 2004.

As already is made clear by this less complex example, in a first step, it is necessary to determine performance indicators pertaining to the material-energetic and cost-related effects of a decision. Moreover, while a number of production-technical parameters may be affected by this decision, they depend on a company context and thus generally cannot be examined. In this regard, an underlying data basis for a flexible performance indicator system has to be created by using the integrated controlling tools (process analysis, material and energy flow accounting, E-ABC). This in turn creates the possibility to generate situation-related information via performance indicators and provide it to the relevant stakeholders, therefore contributing to improving the quality of the decision.

It has been demonstrated that a consistent implementation of the phase model for introducing integrated controlling enables the transparent representation of a multitude of technical-organisational, material-energetic and cost-oriented effects. This representation would not be realisable to its full extent without applying the integrated controlling approach, since such data quality can only be generated via the integration in identical reference objects.

5.4 Summary

An examination of the tools discussed here (material and energy flow accounting, process-oriented costing, performance indicator systems), which can be deployed within the scope of integrated controlling, makes it evident that implementing this type of controlling concept is a complex task. However, since the utilisation of each individual tool brings considerable benefit potentials, a step-by-step introduction results in positive effects at each step and accordingly, the successive implementation of the individual concept components already promises some success. To this end, the phase model described here offers an orientation framework. Furthermore, the industry guidelines provide extensive assistance in demonstrating how integrated controlling can be implemented on the company and operational level of a foundry.[46] The establishment of the decision-making oriented performance indicator model within the scope of integrated controlling sets up the framework for conducting comprehensive causal and impact analyses on the basis of alternative system statuses.

---

[46] See Lange et al. 2003, p. 37

Furthermore, it creates the option of simulating the effects of decisions or measures, thus reducing the risk of making wrong decisions.

It should also be noted here that significant expense and effort is associated with the initial establishment of the material and energy flow accounting as well as the process-oriented environmental activity-based costing and the corresponding performance indicator system. However, this expense and effort is justified by the enhanced transparency and identified saving potentials, which was particularly evidenced in the case studies analysed in the INPROCESS project.

In summary, it can therefore be stated that, in the course of the INPROCESS project, foundry-specific tools were developed and then put to the test and proven in practice. The project therefore contributed to promoting the concept of sustainable management as a state-of-the-art standard in foundries.[47]

---

[47] See Kuchenbuch et al. 2004, p. 28

References

Ahsen A von, Lange Chr (2004) Mehrdimensionale Fehlermöglichkeits- und -einflussanalyse als Instrument des Integrierten Qualitätsmanagements. ZfB 74, pp 441-460

Coenenberg A (2003) Kostenrechnung und Kostenanalyse. vol 5, revised and expanded Edition, Landsberg am Lech

Daldrup H (2002) Externes Umweltschutz-Reporting im Rahmen eines Stakeholderorientierten Controlling. Frankfurt

Deutscher Gießereiverband (1996) Umweltschutzkostenrechnung in Eisen-, Stahl- und Tempergießereien. Ein Branchenleitfaden. Düsseldorf

Dyllick T (1984) Erfassung der Umweltbeziehungen der Unternehmung. Management-Zeitschrift io 53, pp 74-78

Gay J (1998) Stoff- und Energieflusskostenrechnung. Lohmar/ Cologne

Horváth P (2003) Controlling. 9th edn, completely revised Edition. Munich

Kuchenbuch A (2004) Integriertes Controlling in Gießereiunternehmen – Konzeption und prozessbezogene Umsetzung, Beiträge zur Umweltwirtschaft und zum Controlling Nr. 32, University of Duisburg/ Essen, Forthcoming

Kuchenbuch A, Hafkesbrink J, Lange Chr (2004) Kennzahlengestützte Informationsversorgung im Rahmen eines Integrierten Controlling. Umwelt-WirtschaftsForum 12, pp 24-29

Kuchenbuch A, Schroll M, Helber J (2003) Integrierte Kosten- und Stoffflussrechnung in Gießereien. Teil 2: Stoff- und Energieflussrechnung im Rahmen eines Integrierten Controlling. Giesserei 90, pp 32-37

Landesanstalt für Umweltschutz Baden Württemberg (1999) Betriebliches Material- und Energieflussmanagement. Karlsruhe

Lange Chr, Ahsen von A, Daldrup H (2001) Umweltschutz-Reporting. Umwelterklärungen und -berichte als Module eines Reportingsystems. Munich Vienna

Lange Chr, Ahsen von A, Kuchenbuch A (2002) IT-gestütztes Umweltreporting - dargestellt am Beispiel der Georg Fischer GmbH, Mettmann -. UmweltWirtschaftsForum 10, pp 32-36

Lange Chr, Kuchenbuch A (2003) Integrierte Kosten- und Stoffflussrechnung in Gießereien. Teil 1: Umsetzung eines Integrierten Controlling. Giesserei 90, pp 26-33

Lange Chr, Kuchenbuch A (2003a) Integrierte Kosten- und Stoffflussrechnung in Gießereien. Teil 3: Prozessorientierte Kosten- und Stoffflussrechnungen in Gießereien. Giesserei 90, pp 24-33

Lange Chr, Kuchenbuch A, Marzian W (2003) Integrierte Kosten- und Stoffflussrechnung in Gießereien. Teil 4: Prozessorientierte Kosten- und Stoffflussrechnungen in Gießereien. Giesserei 90, pp 32-37

Lange Chr, Schaefer S, Daldrup H (2001) Integriertes Controlling in Strategischen Unternehmensnetzwerken. Controlling 13, pp 75-83

Lange Chr, Martensen O (2003) Wertorientierung des Kostenmanagement. ZfCM 47, pp 259-263

Miller J, Vollmann T (1985) The Hidden Factory. Harvard Business Review 63, pp 142-150

Pfohl H-C, Stölzle W (1991) Anwendungsbedingungen, Verfahren und Beurteilung der Prozeßkostenrechnung in industriellen Unternehmen. ZfB, 61, pp 1281-1305

Pohl I (2001) Investitionsentscheidungen unter Berücksichtigung des Einflusses ökologischer Anspruchsgruppen. Frankfurt/ Main

Rebhan A (1999) Product and Production Integrated Environmental Production and MEAS. (Presentation at the Kansai Research Institute (KRI), 26/11/99)

Rebhan A (2000) Mit Stoff- und Energiemanagement die Kosten bei Stoff- und Energiebezug senken. Verein Industrieller Großkraftwerksbetreiber (VIK)

Reichmann T (2001) Controlling mit Kennzahlen und Managementberichten. 6th revised and expanded edition, Munich

Schaefer S (2001) Integriertes Controlling – Entwicklung einer an Stakeholderinteressen ausgerichteten Controllingkonzeption, Beiträge zur Umweltwirtschaft und zum Controlling. no 22, University of Duisburg/ Essen

Schweitzer M, Küpper H-U (2003) Systeme der Kosten- und Erlösrechnung, 8th edn, Munich

Strobel M, Wagner B (1999) Flusskostenrechnung bei der Firma Merckle-Ratiopharm. Tagungsband zum Management-Symposium „Betriebliche Umweltinformationssysteme in der Praxis", Stuttgart

Sturm A (2000) Performance Measurement und Environmental Performance Measurement. Dissertation, University of Dresden

Verein Deutscher Giessereifachleute (2001) Gießerei 2010 – Strategie für die deutsche Gießereiindustrie. Düsseldorf

6 Environmental Accounting Instruments: Implementation & Continuous Use – Concepts for the Application of Input-Output Balance, Environmental Performance Indicators and Flow Cost Accounting

Claus Lang-Koetz, Thomas Loew, Severin Beucker, Michael Steinfeldt, Uwe Horstmann, Till Sieghart

Claus Lang-Koetz, Institute for Human Factors and Technology Management (IAT), University of Stuttgart, Germany
E-mail: claus.lang-koetz@iao.fraunhofer.de

Thomas Loew, Institute for Ecological Economy Research, Berlin/ Germany
E-Mail: thomas.loew@ioew.de

Severin Beucker, Fraunhofer Institute for Industrial Engineering (IAO), Stuttgart/ Germany
E-Mail: severin.beucker@iao.fraunhofer.de

Michael Steinfeldt, Institute for Ecological Economy Research, Berlin/ Germany
Email: michael.steinfeldt@ioew.de

Uwe Horstmann, Conti Temic Microelectronic GmbH, Nürnberg/ Germany
Email: uwe.horstmann@temic.com

Till Sieghart, Conti Temic Microelectronic GmbH, Nürnberg/ Germany
E-Mail: till.sieghart@temic.com

6.1 Introduction

Within the scope of the three-year research project INTUS, concepts were developed for facilitating the introduction of controlling tools into the internal environmental management systems of enterprises. The new concepts relate to the three key problems with which companies are faced when striving to optimise the internal provision of information in regards to environment-oriented management. Areas to be considered here include (i) the suitability of the various environmental accounting tools, (ii) the provision of the tools by way of information technology, and (iii) the organisational implementation during the introductory phase and in long-term utilisation.

6.2 Research Project INTUS

One of the classic challenges of controlling is the efficient provision of information at the right time, in an appropriate volume in regards to the task at hand and in a suitable format. Environmental accounting, being a sub-function of environmental management in corporate practice, is faced with this challenge as well.[1]

Today, environmental accounting has access to a wide variety of tools. The most important of these include product life-cycle assessments, corporate input-output balances, environmental performance indicators, various environmental activity-based costing approaches as well as a multitude of ecological assessment methods.

The product life-cycle assessment approaches, which initially showed a quite significant amount of variation, have been unified in the meantime; the methodological framework is described in four ISO standards (ISO 14040 to ISO 14043). In principle, it is known in which cases and with what software support a practical application of product life-cycle assessments and similar approaches is possible.

Up to now, the situation was different concerning tools for supporting production-related environmental management. In this area, corporate input-output balances[2], environmental performance indicators[3] and flow cost accounting (a highly promising environmental cost management approach[4]) have long since been recommended as particularly promising tools. All three tools support corporate environmental management and share the common feature of contributing to economically favourable environmental protection measures. However, a closer examination has not been conducted in regards to the interrelationship(s) of these tools or in

---

[1] See Loew, Beucker et al. 2002

[2] See e.g. Hallay, Pfriem 1992; Bundesumweltministerium/ Federal Ministry for the Environment, Umweltbundesamt/ Federal Environmental Agency 1995

[3] See e.g. Landesanstalt für Umweltschutz/ State Institute for Environmental Protection 1997, ISO 14031

[4] See e.g. Strobel 2001; Fichter, Loew et al 1997

terms of whether an environmental performance indicator system or the flow cost accounting method is best applied to which specific case and whether these tools have the potential of replacing corporate input-output balances.[5] Up to now, the question of which information technology solutions are capable of providing efficient and suitable support for these tools has largely remained unanswered. In spite of the ever-increasing efficiency, performance and user-friendliness of business administration software systems, most enterprises still use simple spreadsheets for managing environment-related quantity information, such as indicators.[6] In the end, systematic use of the environmental accounting tools examined here is comparatively rare, despite all the existing guidelines and manuals.

Against this background, the research project INTUS – Operationalisation of Environmental Accounting Instruments through the Effective Use of Environmental Management Information Systems – was initiated. The project was made possible through funding by the BMBF (Bundesministerium für Bildung und Forschung/ Federal Ministry of Education and Research, Förderkennzeichen/ Reference No. 01RU0009). Scientific research project partners include the IAT (Institut für Arbeitswissenschaft und Technologiemanagement/ Institute for Human Factors and Technology Management) at the University of Stuttgart, Germany, the IÖW gGmbH (Institut für ökologische Wirtschaftsforschung/ Institute for Ecological Economy Research) in Berlin, and the Fraunhofer IAO (Institut für Arbeitswirtschaft und Organisation/ Institute for Industrial Engineering.[7] The research project examined the following three areas, along with the resulting research questions:

- *Environmental Accounting Tools:* What is/ are the interrelationship(s) between the input-output balance, environmental performance indicators and flow cost accounting tools and how can the tools be appropriately combined? What specific tool combination should be recommended for which cases?
- *Information Technology Support:* How can the environmental accounting tools be efficiently provided in the long term? Which informational solutions are particularly suitable? What role do Environmental Management Information Systems (EMIS) play?
- *Organisational Integration:* How can organisational barriers be overcome when introducing the environmental accounting tools?

---

[5] See Loew, Jürgens 1999
[6] See Beucker et al 2002; Kottmann, Loew et al 1999
[7] For more information of the project, also refer to
    http://www.bum.iao.fraunhofer.de/intus/

The concepts for addressing these questions were developed within the framework of the scientific key project as well as within the scope of implementation projects in co-operation with four pilot companies: SCHOTT Glas, Continental Teves AG & Co oHG/ Continental Temic Microelectronic GmbH, Alfred Göhring GmbH & Co and Ensinger Mineral-Heilquellen GmbH (Figure 6.1.). At these companies, the pertinent required environmental accounting tools were permanently integrated into the existing information management system.[8]

6.3 Combination of Tools

In a retrospective examination of pilot projects conducted in the 1990s, which dealt with environmental performance indicators and flow cost accounting, the IÖW found that in the companies for which an environmental performance indicator system had been implemented, all relevant eco-efficiency potentials had been identified. Thus, additional implementation of the flow cost accounting method would not have resulted in the identification of further potentials. On the other hand, not only was the costing adjusted in the flow cost accounting projects, but environmental performance indicators were introduced as well. These experiences indicate an overlapping between the two instruments and require a systematic comparison.

For this comparison, two fundamentally different application situations first have to be differentiated between. On the one hand, the one-time application within the scope of analyses has to be examined, on the other hand the ongoing utilisation of the pertinent tool for management and controlling purposes needs to be investigated.

---

[8] An overview of the activities conducted in the pilot companies can be found in the INTUS research project brochure (Spath/ Lang/ Loew 2003); the brochure is available on the Internet at www.bum.iao.fraunhofer.de/downloads and www.ioew.de.

INTUS
Research Project

Operationalisation of Environmental Accounting Instruments through the Effective Use of Environmental Management Information Systems (EMIS)

Tool Application	Information Technology Support	Organisational Integration
What are the interrelationships between the input-output balance, environmental performance indicator and flow cost accounting tools? How can they be appropriately combined?	How can the tools be efficiently supported by information technology? What is the role of environmental management information systems in this context?	How can organisational obstacles be overcome when introducing the tools?
In regards to the continuous support of environmental management,	EMIS for environmental management are well-suited for analysing and modelling material and energy flows at regular intervals.	To be taken into account are (with varying importance over the course of time)
• input-output balances are a standard tool that should be applied every 1 to 3 years,	Functions already provided by most ERP systems can be utilised at minimum effort for the integration of environmental performance indicators and corporate input-output balances. This may require an expansion of the data basis.	• know-how in regards to environmental accounting tools, • IT support and integration, and • the organisational learning capability of the company
• environmental performance indicators are a standard tool for supporting ongoing controlling, strategic considerations and external communication, and		The process outcome depends on the efficient integration of the various stakeholders and their respective tasks into the project implementation and an objective-specific application of organisational learning methods.
• flow cost accounting is a specialised tool only suitable for enterprises featuring specific characteristics with respect to material value, size and production structure.	Due to widespread use in enterprises and the user-specific application options, the use of ERP systems significantly contributes to the organisational integration of the tools.	The process should be designed in a benefit-oriented manner, i.e. it should be possible to terminate it if the expected benefit does not justify organisational embedding.

Query tool in SAP R/3 for preparing the input side of the **input-output balance** and for flexible consumption quantity queries concerning environmentally relevant process materials.

Utilised by the environmental officer at the Nuremberg site for complying with reporting obligations and for preparing analyses; expansion within Temic sites is planned.

Integration of performance indicators in regards to mineral water consumption into the ERP system.

Creation of a flow cost analysis based **decision-making support tool** in Excel; utilised by Production Manager and Head of Logistics.

Corporate **material and energy accounting in Navision Financials** with external environmental performance indicator assessment; wood efficiency performance indicator system in Microsoft Excel; implementation in Navision in 2003/04.

Organisational embedding into corporate environmental management and important production processes.

Implementation of **environmental performance indicator system in SAP R/3** with organisational embedding in corporate environmental management.

Utilised in various company segments, rollout planned at other SCHOTT sites.

I·A·T Institut Arbeitswissenschaft und Technologiemanagement Universität Stuttgart

Institut für ökologische Wirtschaftsforschung gGmbH iöw

Fraunhofer Institut Arbeitswirtschaft und Organisation

FUNDED BY
Bundesministerium für Bildung und Forschung

Fig. 6.1. Research project INTUS

Many examples of successful cost-cutting or risk-reducing environmental protection measures described in the literature are based on results that were realised during the introductory phase and thus with the first-time application of the tools. However, these successful results do not recur to the same extent if the tools are continuously applied. Nevertheless, continuous availability of the appropriate environmental accounting tools is of significant importance, since it is a prerequisite for achieving a continuous reduction in environmental impact. Continuous monitoring of resource consumption developments is the only means of identifying, e.g., production failures, inefficient use of material or the impact of changed production programmes on the material flows. A systematic comparison of the three examined tools and their continuous application in regards to supporting environmental management tasks shows that a combination of corporate input-output balances and environmental performance indicators is well-suited for meeting these tasks (Table 6.1). Flow cost accounting can *only* be a supplement that opens up additional, purely economic benefits.

Table 6.1. Suitability of the input-output balance, environmental performance indicators and flow cost accounting tools for supporting environmental management tasks.[9]

Environmental Management Tasks (and other benefits, italicised)	Corporate Input-Output Balance	Environmental Performance Indicators	Flow Cost Accounting
Determination of relevant environmental aspects	●	○	○
Opening up direct cost-cutting environmental relief potentials – one-time measures	●	●	●
Opening up cost-neutral environmental relief potentials – one-time measures	●	●	○
Support for continuous measures/ facilitation of continuous improvement processes	○	●	▸

---

[9] Source: Loew 2003

Table 6.1. (Cont.)

Identification of environmental performance developments	◗	●	◗
Legal Compliance	○	●	○
Provision of information for environmental reporting	●	●	○
Support in meeting reporting requirements stipulated by authorities	○	●	○
Improvement of costing capacity	○	○	●
Identification of purely cost-cutting potentials (without environmental protection component)	○	○	●

Legend:
● — Clear benefit potential for tool application
◗ — Limited benefit potential
○ — No or marginal benefit potential

Contrary to the situation at the start of the research project INTUS, where the performance indicator and flow cost accounting tools were viewed as equal alternatives, it has now been analytically proven that the flow cost accounting method alone, without performance indicators and input-output balance, is not sufficient for appropriately supporting environmental management. Since the permanent implementation of flow cost accounting, which is principally realised via a corresponding expansion of the existing *costing* functionalities, generates significantly higher expenses and efforts and requires considerably more expert knowledge than the introduction of an environmental performance indicator system, it is only a viable alternative for companies with production structures for which a considerable reduction in material losses can be constantly achieved by way of continuous provision of flow cost information.

As a rule, this is the case for companies with complex material flows and high material losses. A checklist for determining whether a permanent implementation of the flow cost accounting method is a viable alternative was developed by Loew (2003: 25 et seq.).

In most cases, particularly for small and medium-sized enterprises and companies with comparatively *easily manageable and concise* material flows, a one-time analysis utilising the flow cost accounting approach may be helpful, however, for continuous controlling purposes, environmental performance indicators are more suitable and easier to implement.

The analysis of the tools demonstrates that the corporate input-output balance and the corporate environmental performance indicators are standard tools which should be adapted to suit each company's circumstances. Environmentally oriented management should integrate the deployment of these tools into the environmental management system as well as into the various business processes. The recommendation here is to prepare an environmental input-output balance on a regular basis every one to three years in order to identify environmentally relevant trends and periodically audit the current assessment of the environmentally relevant aspects of the company. The environmental performance indicator system primarily serves the purposes of real-time monitoring and controlling of relevant material flows and energy consumption. Depending on the options for employee interaction, this can facilitate efficient resource management. Moreover, the performance indicators ideally trigger improvement suggestions. In addition to this operational control information, a performance indicator system should also provide information about mid-term and long-term trends such as, e.g., energy consumption developments or climate-impacting gas emissions.

Flow cost accounting can be viewed as a specialised tool that, under certain conditions, can be a valuable extension of the existing costing. If a flow cost accounting system is implemented, the flow cost information/ assumes some (but not all!) of the tasks of the environmental performance indicator system.

6.4 Information Technology Support Concept

The developed concept shows what basic information technology solutions exist for supporting the environmental accounting tools and which solutions can be recommended based on the current state of development. When examining the various alternatives, in a process analogous to assessing the tools, a differentiation first has to be made between one-time analyses and the continuous application of the environmental accounting tools. Tools to be considered for one-time analyses are usually spreadsheet applications as well as environmental management information systems (EMIS) for material flow management. EMIS for material flow management are software systems that enable the recording and evaluation of material and energy flows either in regards to specific balance areas or system boundaries, e.g. processes or organisational units, or based on the products that are the source of these material and energy flows.[10]

The following basic solution approaches can be used for the continuous information technology (IT) application of environmental accounting tools: (i) utilisation of spreadsheet or database software (adapted if necessary), (ii) utilisation of EMIS for material flow management, (iii) ERP-integrated solutions, and (iv) intranet-based solutions.

In many cases, companies deploy simple *solutions utilising Office applications* such as Microsoft Excel or Microsoft Access[11] for the purposes of IT supported environmental management. These are often isolated solutions used on local workplace computers. Using macros and Visual Basic for Application (VBA) to adapt and expand the corresponding Microsoft Office products for the specific application cases is a commonly used practice. Usually, the applications are used for data processing and analysis, for example in waste management, for hazardous substances management purposes or when determining performance indicators.

At each of the four pilot companies within the scope of the INTUS research project, *ERP-integrated solutions* have proven to be successful in regards to the continuous application of environmental accounting tools. The conventional task of ERP systems (Enterprise Resource Planning systems) in enterprises lies in fully or partially mapping the processes within a company and thus supporting corporate activities, such as the movement and transformation of goods during the production processes. They are geared towards the product structure and support the management of production, logistics and sales as well as finances, human resources, etc. The following aspects of ERP-integrated solutions were decisive factors for the companies:

- The functionality and scalability of ERP systems have significantly increased during the past years, so that company-specific adaptations can be applied with increasing ease and at reasonable expense and effort.
- ERP-integrated solutions can internally access a multitude of data. This decreases redundancies in the data basis, reduces data inconsistencies and minimises data maintenance expenses and effort. Moreover, only a few interfaces are required.

---

[10] The term EMIS is used synonymously with respect to EMIS for material flow management here; see Schmidt and Keil 2001 and Möller 2000. Examples include software products Audit, Umberto or Gabi.

[11] See Beucker et al. 2002

- In principle, the efforts involved in maintaining an integrated solution and subsequently adapting it to new business or IT requirements, if necessary, are lower than with isolated solutions.
- The company has already amassed the know-how for utilising the ERP systems. Training measures are only required for the new functionalities and these measures can be conducted by in-house specialists.

We consider the advantages of ERP-integrated solutions identified at the pilot companies to be universally applicable. According to the current state of technology, an ERP-integrated solution should therefore be recommended for the majority of companies that want to introduce environmental accounting tools and already currently deploy an ERP system.

Another question examined during the project concerned the way in which *EMIS for material flow management* can be utilised for supporting the environmental accounting tools. Accordingly, an EMIS for material flow management was used on a test basis in all four pilot companies for the purpose of analysing the production and/ or individual production areas. However, it became apparent in each of the four cases that for the continuous application of environmental accounting tools, ERP-integrated solutions are superior to solutions utilising EMIS for material flow management.[12] Reasons for this included, among others, the relatively extensive effort involved in interlinking ERP systems and EMIS as compared to an integrated solution as well as the fact that the functions supplied by the ERP system were sufficient for deploying the tools in the actual cases.

However, it is expected that in the future, the interlinking of EMIS for material flow management and ERP systems will be a simpler task requiring less effort. The initial groundwork for this was done in the research project CARE[13] by developing a Publicly Available Specification (PAS) concerning the transfer of environmentally relevant data from ERP systems to EMIS for material flow management (DIN 2003). This method still has to be tested in practice, but it may lead to a broader application of EMIS for material flow management.

As modelling tools, EMIS for material flow management are well suited for one-time analyses of material and energy flows, generating scenarios, and "what if" analyses. Moreover, they support a methodical, systematic

---

[12] However, there are indicators that EMIS for material flow management might be an interesting production planning and execution solution for sectors with both very homogeneous and high-volume material flows, such as, e.g., foundries or breweries. In such cases, the EMIS would be used too provide the tools.

[13] See Busch et al. 2004

procedural approach for carrying out material flow analyses and material flow accounting.

In general, small and medium-sized enterprises do not have an ERP system. However, they often utilise a network-based IT structure via *the use of an intranet* for supplying information and data files.[14] An intranet is a private data network deploying technologies used in the public Internet.[15] During the research project INTUS, an environmental accounting intranet prototype was developed that facilitates the integration and consolidation of environmental information supplied by various applications which then is made easily accessible to the various users.[16] This intranet solution is geared primarily towards small and medium-sized enterprises that do not have ERP systems. Due to its modular design, which uses ordinary IT resources and technologies, this prototype is an easy to implement option for jointly maintaining and presenting environmental and business information in an integrated, user-focused approach.

6.5 The Challenge of Organisational Integration

As a third focus, the research project INTUS examined the issue of the organisational integration of tools and the interrelationship of this process to environmentally-oriented organisational learning processes. In order to investigate this question, an extensive phase concept for the implementation and institutionalisation of environmental accounting tools was developed within the scope of the project; the concept also strongly incorporated the experiences of the four implementation projects.[17]

The term *institutionalisation* clarifies that this concept does not constitute yet another "implementation guideline" for a specific tool, rather, it has a much wider scope, aiming at avoiding the dilemma of numerous research projects that conclude with the development of a prototypical solution that is not (yet) institutionalised in the company's organisation. Key questions arising from continuous application, such as the issues of expected long-term benefits or the effort and expenses incurred in maintaining the tool are anticipated in the overall concept.

Apart from the absolute benefit, decisive factors for the successful deployment of an environmental accounting tool in a company comprise

---

[14] See Spath 2003
[15] See Kyas 1997
[16] A demo system can be accessed on the Internet at
http://www.bum.iao.fraunhofer.de/uc-intranet
[17] See Steinfeldt, Lang 2004

the effort and expenses incurred in implementing the tool as well as the subsequent organisational effort and ongoing expenses for maintaining the functionality of the tool solution. The phase concept for implementing and institutionalising the environmental accounting tools was developed with the objective of reducing the efforts inherent in these two categories. This process is understood as an organisational innovation, since it becomes apparent that many of the findings generated by business innovation research are transferable. Reflecting numerous phase and promoter models for business innovation processes, the phase concept developed within the project is oriented on the four-phase model for the institutionalisation of organisational innovations developed by Tolbert and Zucker (1996), since this phase model appropriately considers the often neglected topic of organisational sedimentation in enterprises.

Generation of ideas: this phase comprises the search for and pre-selection of ideas. In our context, the actual invention does not lie in inventing new environmental accounting tools, but rather in generating ideas with regards to company-specific adaptations and the organisational introduction and embodiment in enterprises, taking into an account adequate IT support.

Specific problem solution: based on detail analyses, this phase comprises both the development of possibly several specific problem solving alternatives and the prototypical test run of the preferred solution.

Implementation: The implementation phase can be viewed as the development of general, shared meanings of the adapted attitudes and processes which permits an "allocation" of actions. Here, the institutional character of the innovation already becomes visible in defined, but still informal structures. In our case, this phase comprises the organisational embodiment via the definition of tasks and responsibilities and their implementation into the company's operational and organisational structure, including the realisation of the supporting IT solution.

Routine application: sedimentation is complete when the attitudes are established as "given structures" (formal structures) and processes are characterised by routine and non-dependency on specific individuals. In the case of environmental accounting tools, this means that they are routinely utilised within the scope of corporate environmental accounting and that necessary adaptations/ further developments of tools and/ or IT infrastructure are carried out. On the one hand, these four phases (see also Figure 6.2.) sufficiently structure the entire process, while on the other, there is enough room left for further detailing, in order to shape the individual innovation process phases.

By way of integrating the concepts developed during the research project, the following tasks are systematically integrated into an overall process and brought to a methodologically optimal solution within the scope of the phase concept for implementing and institutionalising the environmental accounting tools:

- development of a company-specific, adapted tool solution,
- development of a suitable supporting IT solution,
- company-specific organisational implementation of the developed overall solution, and
- the organisational institutionalisation of the utilisation and benefits of the tool solution into the company's operational and organisational structure.

In accordance with their roles, the experts comprising the largely interdisciplinary project team are actively involved in the individual work and learning processes. Moreover, for an optimal process design, it appears highly practical to give varying weight to the various dimensions of organisational learning in the individual process phases. During the first two phases, generation of ideas/ selection of tools and specific problem solving, learning is first and foremost an individual and/or project group specific process, whereas the implementation and routine application phases are strongly marked by organisational learning.

Moreover, the concept intentionally allows for decision-making situations as well as termination options – in case it becomes obvious within the scope of the analyses that the benefit to be expected does not justify a continuous implementation and organisational embodiment of the environmental accounting tools.

The developed phase concept allows enterprises to implement and institutionalise environmental accounting tools into their organisational structure by way of optimised learning processes.

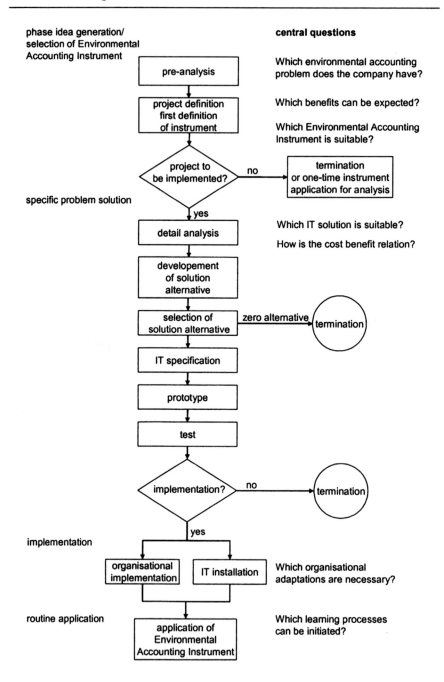

phase idea generation/
selection of Environmental
Accounting Instrument

central questions

pre-analysis

Which environmental accounting
problem does the company have?

project definition
first definition
of instrument

Which benefits can be expected?

Which Environmental Accounting
Instrument is suitable?

project to
be implemented?   no   →   termination
or one-time instrument
application for analysis

specific problem solution

yes

detail analysis

Which IT solution is suitable?

How is the cost benefit relation?

developement
of solution
alternative

selection of
solution alternative   zero alternative   termination

IT specification

prototype

test

implementation?   no   →   termination

yes

implementation

organisational
implementation   IT installation   Which organisational
adaptations are necessary?

routine application

application of
Environmental
Accounting Instrument

Which learning processes
can be initiated?

Fig. 6.2. Phase concept for implementation and institutionalisation of environmental accounting tools (Source: own presentation)

6.6 Case Study: Preparation of Corporate Input-Output Balances and Environmentally Related Consumption Quantity Analyses in SAP R/3

6.6.1 Initial Situation

It already became apparent that corporate environmental management necessitates the collection and management of data and information that, in companies, are usually stored in various different information systems. This was also the case with Continental Temic Microelectronic GmbH. At the Nuremberg (Germany) site, electronic components for the automotive industry are developed and produced. A part of the Continental Automotive Systems (CAS) Group Division, Continental Temic is a Continental AG company based in Hanover, Germany. Production in Nuremberg primarily focuses on the 'Powertrain and Chassis' product segment, e.g., engine management, transmission controls, power electronics and chassis electronics. Since 1996, the site has been using an environmental management system certified in accordance with EMAS and ISO 14001. Up to now, the preparation of a corporate input-output balance or the determination of consumption quantities for the hazardous substances register necessitated individual material numbers or material group queries in the SAP R/3 ERP system. The results were manually transferred into a spreadsheet application. The project at Temic aimed at making the consumption quantity data stored in SAP R/3 accessible to the environmental management. Until now, such queries were not possible because the material groups are organised according to production requirements and thus criteria related to physical material properties, such as, e.g., steel and ferrous materials, thick film pastes, cleaning agents and lyes were only included to a limited amount. At Temic, information regarding consumption quantities related to environmental protection and occupational safety is required for, among other things, preparing a corporate input-output balance, meeting reporting requirements stipulated by environmental legislation[18] 440 2001; BImSchV 31[19] and within the scope of approval management[20]. Moreover, it can also be used for the specific analysis of consumption trends for cost or environmentally

---

[18] TRGS – *Technische Regeln für Gefahrstoffe*/ German Technical Rules for Hazardous Substances

[19] *Bundesimmissionsschutzverordnung*/ German Federal Immission Control Act) 2001

[20] BetrSichV/ *Betriebssicherheitsverordnung*/ German Occupational/ Industrial Safety Regulations 2002

relevant materials, in order to detect undesirable trends in good time and identify potentials for improvement.[21] In the course of the research project INTUS, the IAO and the IÖW, in co-operation with Continental Temic in Nuremberg, have jointly developed a concept that facilitates utilisation of the SAP R/3 corporate information system for preparing a corporate input-output balance as well as for monitoring substance and material consumption relevant to environmental protection and occupational safety. The developed solution comprises a multi-character key as well as query functions which were realised by using the ABAP List Viewer in SAP R/3. The query functions facilitate both pre-defined standard queries as well as individually defined queries. At Temic, the key was named eco key, since its primary field of application is environmental management. Initially, the eco key and the analyses based on it are utilised by the environmental officer at the Nuremberg site. In the future, the plan is to introduce the eco key at all Temic sites and possibly implement it across the entire Continental Automotive Systems (CAS) group division. This would allow cross-locational consumption quantity analyses and efficient preparation of a group division input-output balance.

6.6.2 Realisation of Eco Key in SAP R/3

Eco Key Structure

The developed eco key is a multi-character, alphanumerical, descriptive key that is assigned to the material number maintained in SAP R/3. The key comprises the following characteristics:

- Material type: describes the parts in regards to production technology aspects, such as, e.g., standard parts, drawings, merchandise.
- Chart of accounts key: organises the materials according to the input-output balance systematic. In this context, the materials classification of the VDA[22] was integrated (VDA 1997), which is used by this industrial sector for material composition specifications (Tec4U n/d) example: non-ferrous metals – copper alloys, acids, lyes.
- Environmental properties: assigns environmental properties to the materials, if applicable. Here, a differentiation is made between characteristics of materials that are included in hazardous substances law and specific environmental aspects defined by Temic.

---

[21] See Loew et al. 2002

[22] Verband der Automobilindustrie / *German Association of the Automotive Industry*

The characteristics of the material types and charts of accounts are maintained and stored as an SAP classification in the SAP MM (Material Management) module.

The characteristics of the eco key in regards to environmental properties are not used at this point in time. In order to utilise these characteristics, the SAP EH&S (Environment, Health & Safety) module could possible be used in the future. The environmental properties could be maintained and managed in the specifications. Such a utilisation of SAP EH&S at Temic has not yet been finally decided upon. It also particularly depends on the application of EH&S within the scope of the internal hazardous substances management and the 'International Material Data System'[23] (also see below).

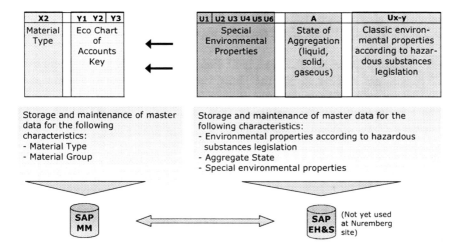

Fig. 6.3. Storage and maintenance of eco key data with characteristic attributes

The eco key used at Temic represents a new approach to the use of environmentally relevant data in SAP R/3. It is interesting in this context that the eco key utilises existing SAP MM data, which are made available to the environmental management for analysis by means of classification and a comparatively simple IT solution.

---

[23] The 'International Material Data System' (IMDS) is the basis of the automotive industry's material data system. All materials used in vehicle construction are archived and managed in IMDS. In particular, IMDS has the task of complying with the EC End of Life Vehicle Directive (on IMDS, see also http://www.imds.de).

Also interesting is the potential arising from the use of SAP EH&S for further analyses of relevant characteristics. This is demonstrated by the deployment of SAP EH&S within the IMDS framework at Temic. In cooperation with a development partner, a module was designed at Continental Automotive Systems and globally introduced that enables efficient processing of materials data in a SAP EH&S environment. Via an XML[24] interface, SAP EH&S can supply product materials data to the IMDS database. The concept developed for an internal materials data management system in EH&S in conjunction with the IMDS database interface is a pilot application in the automotive supplier sector. In the meantime, the application has been offered by the CAS development partners as a sector-specific application for extending SAP EH&S.

6.6.3 IT Related and Organisational Implementation of Eco Key

The implementation of the eco key at Continental Temic necessitated both IT related and organisational measures; these measures were developed in the course of workshops that accompanied the project and then conceptually integrated. In the following, the most important steps of the IT related and organisational implementation of the eco key are described.

IT Related Implementation of Eco Key:

1. Assignment of eco key to material groups: in a one-time assignment procedure, the eco key is assigned to the materials maintained in SAP R/3 with a material number. This was done on a step-by-step basis. First, the keys were assigned to the material groups which are homogeneous from the standpoint of an eco key systematic. This step was carried out by means of a spreadsheet software program.
2. Assignment of eco key to material numbers: wherever an assignment via material groups was not possible, a spreadsheet software program was also used for directly assigning the keys to material numbers and thus directly to individual materials in inhomogeneous material groups.
3. Upload of assignment table to SAP test system: by utilising ABAP[25] applications, the assignment tables generated in steps 1 and 2 were loaded into the SAP R/3 system and the analyses described in the next

---

[24] XML is a meta-programming language which was developed on the basis of the SGML ISO standard. XML is a W3C standard (see www.w3.org/XML/) and thus company and platform independent.

[25] ABAP applications are software programs created in SAP's proprietary ABAP (Advanced Business and Application Programming) programming language.

section were prepared. First, the assignment tables were loaded into the SAP test system at the Nuremberg site.

4. Setting up material movement types: the movement types defined in SAP R/3 are used for the actual consumption quantity analyses based on the eco key. The SAP system at TEMIC differentiates between a wide variety of movement types, only a part of which need to be considered in order to generate a statement concerning, e.g., consumption. For consumption analyses purposes, the movement types are summarised into the following categories:

   - Inward Movements
   - Consumption
   - Outward Movements
   - Inventory Differences

5. Via these movement categories, double counting when calculating the queries is avoided. This ensures, e.g., that goods receipts are not included in the consumption quantity calculation.

6. Definition of typical queries via the eco key: in order to test the query and analysis options of the eco key, typical queries were defined, such as, e.g., determining the consumption quantity of process materials containing VOC or heavy metals.

7. Trial run on test system: several plausibility and functionality tests were run to test the eco key and the queries realisable via it. In particular, it was possible to remedy incorrect eco key assignments and adjust the material master data.

8. Transfer to the SAP R/3 live system: after extensive testing, the eco key was transferred into the site's SAP R/3 live system.

While the conceptual activities for implementing the eco key were performed by the scientific and research partners and Continental Temic, the software implementation in SAP R/3 was carried out by the internal IT department at Continental Temic. Programming took approx. 5 workdays. In addition, Continental Temic prepared extensive user documentation for working with the eco key.

Organisational Implementation of Eco Key:

After the one-time assignment to the material master data, the eco key should henceforth also be assigned to newly introduced materials. To this end, the workflows for introducing new materials were revised and adjusted. Depending on the material type, procurement can follow different processes. Accordingly, hazardous substance management processes and procurement workflows had to be adjusted within the scope of the organisational implementation of the eco key. At present, eco keys are only assigned to hazardous substances. The procedure is extremely lean and does not necessitate extensive documentation. With the exception of the environmental officer, no other persons have to be involved in handling the eco key.

Each hazardous substance must first be examined by a hazardous substances committee. The approval form was supplemented by the eco key. The environmental officer uses this form when subsequently creating the SAP classification view.

At Continental Temic, the SAP production material master data are centrally created. After creating the data, the relevant organisational units at the plants are requested to maintain the corresponding plant views. In the case of hazardous substances, the environmental officer undertakes the creation of the SAP classification view. The SAP material master data for process materials is locally created by the Purchasing departments at the plants. Here as well, the environmental officer undertakes maintenance of the SAP classification view after the material master data have been created.

Eco Key Supported Analyses

Eco key supported analyses are conducted as flexible queries via the characteristics described in Section 6.6.2. For analysis purposes, all characteristics contained in the eco key can be freely combined and queried for definable periods of time. The ABAP List Viewer is used for the queries. The ABAP List Viewer is an SAP R/3 internal control element for preparing, standardising and displaying listings. The ABAP List Viewer facilitates the user-specific storage of display variants in regards to column formats, sorting criteria and filter conditions. This also makes it possible to create pre-defined queries for, e.g., determining input quantities within the scope of input-output balances.

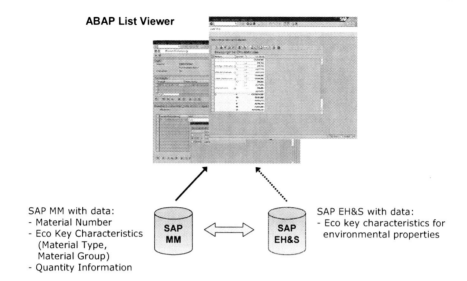

Fig. 6.4. Eco key supported analysis via ABAP list viewer

The analyses carried out via the ABAP list viewer result in total displays of defined consumption areas in the form of lists, which can be exported for further analysis and graphic editing. As shown in figure 6.4, a possible future analysis of data in SAP EH&S was allowed for in the ABAP List Viewer.

6.6.4 Eco Key Usage and Rollout in Group Division

At present, the eco key is used at the Nuremberg site within the scope of a pilot application for the following queries and analyses:

- Preparation of input-output balance: a respective query was realised in the ABAP List Viewer as a fixed setting (see Figure 6.5.). The creation of an input quantity query for future input-output balances at the site can thus be carried out in a much more efficient and timely manner.
- Analysis of consumption trends for environmentally/occupational safety relevant materials: several standard queries were developed for the analysis of the consumption trends of relevant materials. In addition, users can design their own, problem-specific queries in the query module. First and foremost, this function is intended to be utilised for tracking specific consumption quantity trends (e.g. VOC and heavy metals).

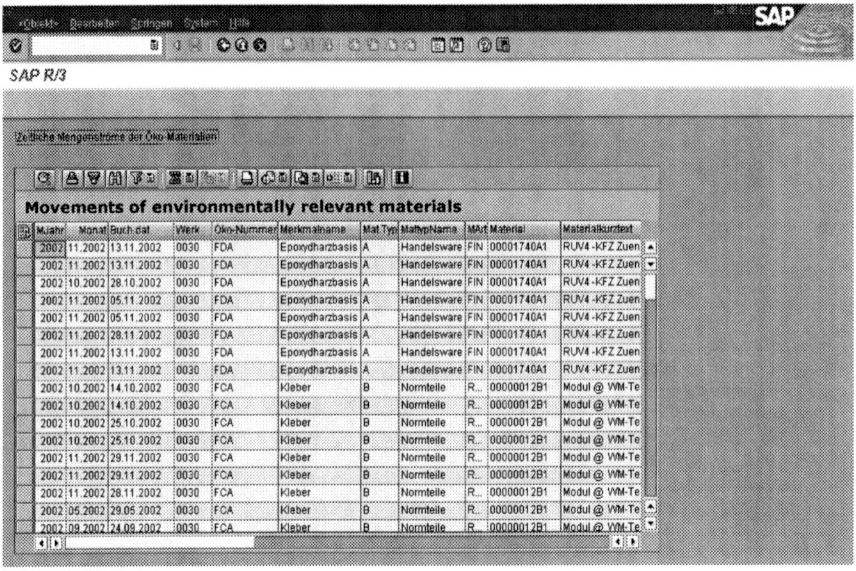

MJahr	Monat	Buch.dat	Werk	Öko-Nummer	Merkmalname	Mat.Typ	MattypName	MArt	Material	Materialkurztext
2002	11.2002	13.11.2002	0030	FDA	Epoxydharzbasis	A	Handelsware	FIN	00001740A1	RUV4 -KFZ Zuen
2002	11.2002	13.11.2002	0030	FDA	Epoxydharzbasis	A	Handelsware	FIN	00001740A1	RUV4 -KFZ Zuen
2002	10.2002	28.10.2002	0030	FDA	Epoxydharzbasis	A	Handelsware	FIN	00001740A1	RUV4 -KFZ Zuen
2002	11.2002	05.11.2002	0030	FDA	Epoxydharzbasis	A	Handelsware	FIN	00001740A1	RUV4 -KFZ Zuen
2002	11.2002	05.11.2002	0030	FDA	Epoxydharzbasis	A	Handelsware	FIN	00001740A1	RUV4 -KFZ Zuen
2002	11.2002	28.11.2002	0030	FDA	Epoxydharzbasis	A	Handelsware	FIN	00001740A1	RUV4 -KFZ Zuen
2002	11.2002	13.11.2002	0030	FDA	Epoxydharzbasis	A	Handelsware	FIN	00001740A1	RUV4 -KFZ Zuen
2002	11.2002	13.11.2002	0030	FDA	Epoxydharzbasis	A	Handelsware	FIN	00001740A1	RUV4 -KFZ Zuen
2002	10.2002	14.10.2002	0030	FCA	Kleber	B	Normteile	R...	00000012B1	Modul @ WM-Te
2002	10.2002	14.10.2002	0030	FCA	Kleber	B	Normteile	R...	00000012B1	Modul @ WM-Te
2002	10.2002	25.10.2002	0030	FCA	Kleber	B	Normteile	R...	00000012B1	Modul @ WM-Te
2002	10.2002	25.10.2002	0030	FCA	Kleber	B	Normteile	R...	00000012B1	Modul @ WM-Te
2002	11.2002	29.11.2002	0030	FCA	Kleber	B	Normteile	R...	00000012B1	Modul @ WM-Te
2002	11.2002	29.11.2002	0030	FCA	Kleber	B	Normteile	R...	00000012B1	Modul @ WM-Te
2002	11.2002	28.11.2002	0030	FCA	Kleber	B	Normteile	R...	00000012B1	Modul @ WM-Te
2002	05.2002	29.05.2002	0030	FCA	Kleber	B	Normteile	R...	00000012B1	Modul @ WM-Te
2002	09.2002	24.09.2002	0030	FCA	Kleber	B	Normteile	R...	00000012B1	Modul @ WM-Te

Fig. 6.5. Result of input analysis with ABAP list viewer

The eco key has yet to be introduced in the Continental Automotive Systems group division. Among other things, it depends on the group-wide usage of SAP EH&S for hazardous substance management purposes as well as the implementation of the material data system (IMDS). Since there is an overlapping of eco key and IMDS characteristics, it is necessary to develop viable solutions on a group-wide basis after introducing IMDS.

6.6.5 Case Study Conclusion

The project conducted at Continental Temic in the course of the research project INTUS demonstrates that ERP systems such as, e.g., SAP R/3 contain extensive information relevant to environmental management, including not only obvious data such as, e.g., hazardous substances, but also consumption quantity related data that is needed for meeting numerous accounting obligations as well as for analysis and monitoring tasks pertaining to corporate environmental management. In many cases, ERP systems also contain basic support features for environmental management tasks, such as, for example, hazardous substances or waste management. However, a targeted accounting for environmentally relevant material consumption and consumption quantities is not possible at present, therefore making ERP systems and the data they contain useless for many corporate environmental management tasks. The project was able to show that data available from ERP systems can be utilised for preparing input-output balances and for conducting flexible analyses of consumption quantity trends for environmentally relevant material components via the implementation of an eco key. Moreover, existing software logic and technology could be used for the IT implementation in SAP R/3, leading to a reduction in the actual programming efforts. The project focused on the conceptual activities required for integrating the requirements specific to environmental management and the supporting IT implementation in a conclusive overall concept.

The implementation of the eco key in SAP R/3 broke new ground in several regards. On the one hand, the eco key represents a new approach to the use of environmentally relevant data in SAP R/3. On the other hand, the application of SAP EH&S for the purposes of corporate hazardous substances management would open up further potentials for eco key based analyses. Moreover, by establishing a reference between material related data and product bills of materials, a step could be taken to progress from site or plant related accounting towards product related accounting, which would enable, e.g., analyses summarised according to specific materials for specific product groups and periods of time. A summary documentation of the materials for a specific product or customer over a certain period of time could also be realised this way – a first step towards preparing a life cycle inventory analysis within the scope of a product life cycle assessment.

The case study also demonstrated that using existing data for environmental management purposes contributes to the efficient provision of information in several ways. For one, the effort and expense in terms of time and human resources for preparing input-output balances and determining consumption quantity trends for specific materials could be significantly reduced. And secondly, the analyses are available to various users and can easily be further utilised in reports. The case study also shows that a high potential for the usage of environmentally relevant data available from ERP systems still exists and that corresponding analyses can be expanded as required.

6.7 Summary and Outlook

When the idea for the research project was developed in 1999, numerous uncertainties existed in regards to the interrelationships between the examined environmental accounting tools. Many hopes focused on the flow cost accounting method, which, as an innovative extension to conventional costing, establishes a link between environmental management and cost controlling. This new approach was perceived to be a chance for gaining more acceptance for environmental management within enterprises and better integrate it into the business processes both in terms of cost reporting and on an organisational level. However, the research project INTUS has demonstrated that a continuous integration of flow cost accounting under the current technical conditions can only recommended for certain enterprises with complex production structures as well as high quantitative and ad valorem material losses. In all other cases, the introduction of environmental performance indicator systems yields a significantly better cost/benefit ratio and is thus preferred.

Deploying the flow cost accounting method for one-time analyses presents a different picture. In this context, pertinent calculations can provide valuable indicators in terms of ecologically and economically interesting efficiency potentials.

At the start of the project, similar uncertainties existed regarding the suitable IT support for providing the environmental accounting tools. Already at that point in time, both researchers and companies expressed a great interest in EMIS for material flow management. At the same time, the already longstanding trend of discontinuing isolated solutions in favour of integrated software systems continued to develop. Large-scale ERP systems are increasingly integrating more functions while simultaneously becoming more flexible, easier to adapt and thus more and more effective.

In view of the current state of the art in regards to software products for the continuous provision of environmental accounting tools, comprising input-output balance, environmental performance indicators and, if necessary, flow cost accounting, the research project has shown that ERP integrated solutions are recommendable. In particular, this is also evidenced by the case study conducted at Continental Temic, during which it was possible to implement, at reasonable cost and effort, an SAP R/3 based support for corporate input-output balance purposes. A prototypical intranet solution was developed for small and medium-sized enterprises that do not utilise an ERP system. Staying on top of further software technology developments is absolutely essential. As soon as the effort and expense involved in integrating EMIS for material flow management is significantly reduced, the competition between ERP integrated solutions and EMIS based solutions will once again become relevant. Therefore, the question as to which approach will prevail in the long term remains unanswered, despite the fact that ERP integrated solutions are currently more suitable for the continuous provision of the environmental accounting tools examined here.

In contrast, EMIS for material flow management have proven themselves as modelling and analysis tools. They display definite strengths in the area of assessing environmental impacts within the scope of corporate balances or life cycle assessments. Since they provide assessment procedures and environmental impact data, they are especially suitable for these tasks and are particularly recommended for consultants or company-internal staff who have mastered the software and are able to efficiently use it.

Finally, many expectations were roused by the research work focused on the development of an organisational concept for integrating the tools. An examination of the theoretical concepts concerning organisational learning, among other things, has fostered the development of a conclusive phase concept, although such theories have contributed less than initially hoped. Nevertheless, a phase concept could be developed that enables enterprises to optimally implement and institutionalise the environmental accounting tools in the internal organisational structure. To this end, the phase concept integrates the concepts dealing with the decision-making process in regards to tool deployment and IT support, which were developed within the scope of the research project.

The fundamental question regarding the cost/benefit ratio of a continuous integration of the respective tools still remains decisive for the prioritisation of corresponding environmental projects. If the net benefit is perceived to be too low, or is actually too low, projects are either cancelled or assigned a low priority in enterprises, which significantly impedes their implementation. For environmental political implications, this seemingly trivial finding leads to the conclusion that an evaluation has to examine in which way(s) the actual and/or perceived benefit of the tools can be increased. Possible starting points may include regulations and voluntary agreements (e.g. reporting) as well as public relations activities.

References

Beucker S, Jürgens G, Lang C, Rey U (2002) Betriebliche Umweltinformationssysteme (BUIS) im Umweltcontrolling – Umfrage zur Nutzung von Instrumenten des Umweltcontrollings und deren informationstechnischen Unterstützung. Arbeitsbericht des IAT, Stuttgart

Bundesumweltministerium, Umweltbundesamt (eds) (1995) Handbuch Umweltcontrolling. Munich

Bundesumweltministerium, Umweltbundesamt (eds) (2001) Handbuch Umweltcontrolling. 2nd edn, Munich

Busch T, Beucker S, Lehmann C (2004) Ressourceneffizienzrechnung in der Mittelständischen Wirtschaft - Ziele und Ergebnisse des care-Projekts. In: Institut der deutschen Wirtschaft Cologne (ed) Betriebliche Instrumente für nachhaltiges Wirtschaften, Konzepte für die Praxis. Cologne (in press)

DIN (ed) (2003) PAS 1025 „Austausch umweltrelevanter Daten zwischen ERP-Systemen und betrieblichen Umweltinformationssystemen". Berlin

DIN EN ISO 14031 (2000) Umweltmanagement, Umweltleistungsbewertung, Leitlinien. Berlin

DIN EN ISO 14040 (1997) Umweltmanagement Ökobilanz, Prinzipien und allgemeine Anforderungen. Berlin

DIN EN ISO 14041 (1998) Umweltmanagement Ökobilanz, Festlegung des Ziels und des Untersuchungsrahmens sowie Sachbilanz. Berlin

DIN EN ISO 14042 (2000) Umweltmanagement Ökobilanz, Wirkungsabschätzung. Berlin

DIN EN ISO 14043 (2000) Umweltmanagement Ökobilanz, Auswertung. Berlin

Fichter K; Loew T; Seidel E (1997) Betriebliche Umweltkostenrechnung, Methoden und praxisgerechte Weiterentwicklung. Berlin Heidelberg New York

Gappmeier M; Heinrich L.-J (eds) (1998) Geschäftsprozesse mit menschlichem Antlitz, Methoden des organisationalen Lernens anwenden. Linz

Hallay H; Pfriem R (1992) Öko-Controlling, Umweltschutz in mittelständischen Unternehmen. Frankfurt New York

Hauschildt J (1997) Innovationsmanagement. Munich

Hennemann C (1997) Organisationales Lernen und die lernende Organisation – Entwicklung eines praxisbezogenen Gestaltungsvorschlages aus ressourcenorientierter Sicht. Munich

Kottmann H; Loew T; Clausen J (1999) Umweltmanagement mit Kennzahlen. Munich

Kyas O (1997) Corporate Intranets: Strategie, Planung. Bonn

Landesanstalt für Umweltschutz Baden- Württemberg (LfU) (ed) (1999) Arbeitsmaterialien zur Einführung von Umweltkennzahlensystemen. Karlsruhe

Loew T; Jürgens G (1999) Flusskostenrechnung versus Umweltkennzahlen- Was ist das richtige Instrument für das betriebliche Umweltmanagement? In: Ökologisches Wirtschaften, no 05- 06/99, Munich

Loew T (2003) Konzept zur Entscheidungsfindung über den Einsatz von betrieblichen Umweltbilanzen, Umweltkennzahlen und Flusskostenrechnung. Arbeitsbericht des IAT, Stuttgart

Loew T, Beucker S, Jürgens G (2002) Vergleichende Analyse der Umweltcontrollinginstrumente- Umweltbilanz, Umweltkennzahlen und Flusskostenrechnung. Arbeitsbericht des IAT und Diskussionspapier des IÖW no 53/02, Berlin

Möller A (2000) Grundlagen stoffstrombasierter betrieblicher Umweltinformationssysteme. Bochum

Nagl A (1997) Lernende Organisation: Entwicklungsstand, Perspektiven und Gestaltungsansätze in deutschen Unternehmen – Eine empirische Untersuchung. Aachen

Probst G; Büchel B (1998) Organisationales Lernen: Wettbewerbsvorteil der Zukunft. 2nd edn, Wiesbaden

Schmidt M, Keil R (2001) Stoffstromnetze und ihre Nutzen für mehr Kostentransparenz sowie die Analyse der Umweltwirkungen betrieblicher Stoffströme. Beiträge der Hochschule Pforzheim, no 103, Pforzheim

Spath D (ed) (2004) Information und Kommunikation in der Produktion – Ergebnisse einer Unternehmensbefragung. Stuttgart

Spath D, Lang C; Loew T. (eds.) 2003 Umweltcontrolling in produzierenden Unternehmen - Ergebnisse aus dem Forschungsprojekt INTUS. Stuttgart Berlin

Steinfeldt M 2003 Organisationales Lernen und umweltbezogene Lernprozesse. Berlin

Steinfeldt M, Lang C (2004) Konzept zur Implementierung und Institutionalisierung von Instrumenten des Umweltcontrolling. Stuttgart Berlin

Strobel M (2001) Systemisches Flussmanagement. Augsburg

Tec4U Ingenieurgesellschaft (ed) Willkommen bei IMDS-Service. (URL: http://www.imds.de/deu/index_d.htm [04/08/03])

TRGS 440 (2001) Technische Regeln für Gefahrstoffe: TRGS 440 - Ermitteln und Beurteilen der Gefährdungen durch Gefahrstoffe am Arbeitsplatz: Ermitteln von Gefahrstoffen und Methoden zur Ersatzstoffprüfung. (URL: http://www.umweltschutzrecht.de/recht/t_regelin/trgs/trgs400/440_ges.htm)

Tolbert P, Zucker L (1996) The Institutionalisation of Institutional Theory. In: Clegg S, Hardy C, Nord W (eds) Handbook of Organization Studies. London, pp 175-190

VDA Verband der Automobilindustrie (ed) (1997) Werkstoffklassifizierung im Kraftfahrzeugbau. Aufbau und Nomenklatur. Frankfurt (URL: http://www.ioew.de and http://www.bum.iao.fraunhofer.de/intus)

7 Efficient Closure of Material and Component Loops –
Substance Flow Oriented Supply Chain Management

Martin Ploog, Wiebke Stölting, Marcus Schröter, Thomas Spengler, Christoph Herrmann, René Graf

Martin Ploog, Institute of Business Administration, Department of Production Management, Technical University of Braunschweig, Germany
E-Mail: m.ploog@tu-bs.de

Wiebke Stölting, Institute of Business Administration, Department of Production Management, Technical University of Braunschweig, Germany
E-Mail: w.stoelting@tu-bs.de

Marcus Schröter, Institute of Business Administration, Department of Production Management, Technical University of Braunschweig, Germany
E-Mail: marcus.schroeter@tu-bs.de

Thomas Spengler, Institute of Business Administration, Department of Production Management, Technical University of Braunschweig, Germany
E-Mail: t.spengler@tu-bs.de

Christoph Herrmann, Institute of Machine Tools and Production Technology, Department of Production and Life-Cycle-Management, Technical University of Braunschweig, Germany
E-Mail: c.herrmann@tu-bs.de

René Graf, Institute of Machine Tools and Production Technology, Department of Production and Life-Cycle-Management, Technical University of Braunschweig, Germany
E-Mail: r.graf@tu-bs.de

7.1 Introduction

In view of the integration of product stewardship into environmental law and the accompanying task faced by manufacturers in taking back and recycling products at the end of their service lives, existing logistics chains (supply chains) need to be extended to include the after-use phase. Linking a supply chain with the after-use phase of the product creates a substance flow oriented supply chain. The goal of such a substance flow oriented supply chain management is to design and co-ordinate all company functions and processes in a way that enables closing the flow of goods and materials while at the same time cost-efficiently meeting customer service objectives. In this regard, the resultant co-operation between manufacturers and recycling companies can on the one hand fulfill future legal requirements and on the other exploit existing economic potentials that arise from efficiently planned take-back of used equipment and its recycling. Up to now, such expanded supply chains have only rarely been found in practice. For this reason, an integrated concept is needed that takes into account both the strategic and operative planning levels as well as the information management for the expanded supply chain. Such a comprehensive concept was developed in the BMBF[1] funded project *StreaM – Substance Flow Oriented Closed Loop Supply Chain Management in the Electrical and Electronic Equipment Industry* and validated over the course of several case studies. Selected results from these will be presented in this paper.

Partners in the substance flow oriented supply chain especially include manufacturers and recycling companies. Within the scope of the co-operation, the manufacturer takes on the position of the focal company, assuming a managerial role and co-ordinating the cross-company task allocation process.[2] The recycling company recycles the used equipment in a co-operative collaboration with the manufacturer, with the disassembly and processing subareas playing a particularly important role.

To ensure the economic and ecological advantageousness of recovery systems, efficient closed loop strategies have to be identified and pursued in the future. While numerous approaches for systematising possible closed loop strategies can be found in the literature[3], they are frequently inconsistent. Thus, in the StreaM project, a systematisation method was

---

[1] Bundesministerium für Bildung und Forschung/ Federal Ministry of Education and Research
[2] See Picot et al. 2003
[3] Gungor and Gupta, 1999, provide an overview of such systematisation approaches.

developed that complies with future regulations for electrical and electronic devices (EC directive 2002/96/EC 2003) and enables closed loop strategies to be allocated to value-added phases. The value-added phases are therefore sub-divided on the basis of the product structure (see Figure 7.1.).

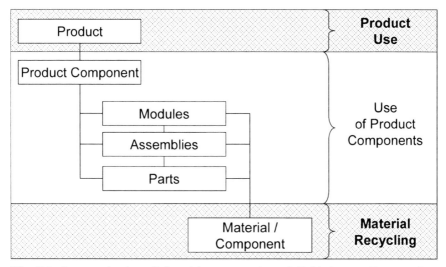

Fig. 7.1. Systematisation of closed loop strategies subdivided according to value-added phases

For implementing the material recycling strategy, the form and shape of the product or product components are completely destroyed in the course of the treatment process. Recycling can then take the form of material or thermal recycling. A closed loop strategy that does not destroy the shape/ form of the product or product components and re-uses their functional properties is called *re-use*. To differentiate the value-added levels on which re-use occurs, the terms *product re-use* and *product component re-use* are utilised.

The identification and exploitation of the hidden potentials of closed loop strategies with respect to a sustainable substance flow oriented supply chain economy requires suitable planning tools that support decision-making.

On the manufacturer's side, it is particularly essential to develop strategic tools for evaluating the closed loop strategies. For the recycling companies, the development of a planning environment is required, which enables efficient operative planning based on the information provided by the manufacturer. Furthermore, business processes for closing material loops have to be designed within the scope of an inter-company co-operation, resulting in the project structure shown in figure 7.2.

Fig. 7.2. Work packages of the StreaM project

The project was conducted within the scope of a research association comprising the Institute of Business Administration, Department of Production Management, and the Institute of Machine Tools and Production Technology at the TU Braunschweig in conjunction with the Electrocycling GmbH (Goslar/ Germany) and Agfa-Gevaert AG (Munich/ Germany) industrial partners.

This paper will describe the concept and planning tools for the extended supply chain that were developed over the course of the project, including the partner companies, and discuss their advantageousness by means of case studies. The focus lies on the developed information flow concept as well as on the implementation of strategies for the re-use of product components.

This paper is structured as follows: following an introduction to the procedure for the practical realisation of the concept in application-oriented case studies, the implementation of the information concept will be discussed in Section 7.3. Based on the provided product information, the implementation of a case study on material recycling will be presented in Section 7.4. Section 7.5 will then elaborate in detail on the re-use of product components as a second closed loop strategy and the expansion of the information concept it requires. In this context, the use of components for the purpose of supplying spare parts is identified as a very promising option. One possibility for its implementation is subsequently described in Section 7.6. The paper concludes with an outlook (Section 7.7) and a summary (Section 7.8).

7.2 Procedure for Practical Realisation

The first step in the exemplary application of the tools developed in the project was to select various products from the Agfa-Geavert AG product spectrum. In consideration of the technical, logistical and economic criteria, the ADC product family was selected. The ADC Compact, ADC Compact Plus and ADC Solo are currently being produced, with the ADC Compact being phased out and the successor products in production start-up. As the predecessor model, the ADC 70 is being replaced by many customers and is thus particularly relevant from a recycling standpoint.

The ADC products are Computed Radiography (CR) systems and *digitizers*. The digitizers process the data from the x-rays into digital images, which are then sent via networks within the hospital or to recipients on worldwide basis. The ADC products scan the exposed ADC imaging plates, convert the information into digital data and automatically transmit the images to the image processing computers for editing and visualisation. The ADC imaging plates can then be re-used again for new exposures.

From January 1st to October 1st 2003, all used devices were collected by Electrocycling GmbH. During this period, a total of three ADC 70s could be taken back, and since these products were still in good condition, analyses could be conducted on them. The ADC 70s were systematically disassembled for two reasons. For one, the recycling-relevant testing of the developed planning methodology had to be performed and secondly, the product components were recovered for re-use. Furthermore, the developed information flow concept had to be tested and validated by way of example. After the analyses had been conducted and the product components removed, the remaining used equipment and parts were properly recycled by the Electrocycling GmbH specialists.

The product components recovered and analysed within the scope of the re-use case study were then sent back to Agfa-Gevaert AG for the purpose of validating their condition and reusability. For the duration of the service period guaranteed to the customer, Agfa-Gevaert AG stores essential and specific operating/ technical equipment for the production and testing of the devices, such as e.g. specific appliances and handling equipment, in case that spare parts have to be reproduced or redesigned. The test devices and testing software for the ADC 70 are therefore still available. After the software had been successfully reactivated, the used components were tested. It turned out that, although the remaining service lives could not be accurately determined, the parts were functional. The parts were labelled as used product components, the parent device history was identified and the parts were handed over to the spare parts central warehouse. There, the parts are kept as an additional availability option in case the remaining stock is not sufficient. Since the product components have been proven functioning, the closed loop supply chain is successfully closed.

7.3 Implementation of Information Concept

The objective of the concept is to provide suitable approaches for a communication platform for the partners (manufacturers and recycling companies) involved in the substance flow oriented supply chain. In addition to meeting the legal requirements concerning the provision of information, this also enables decision-making and planning support for the supply chain partners. To this end, an inter-company communication platform was created that interlinked the product development phase with the after-use phase and is based on the recycling passport approach developed by Agfa-Gevaert AG (see Figure 7.3).

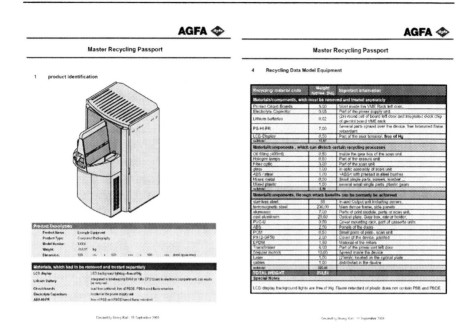

Fig. 7.3. Sample first and last page of a recycling passport

The recycling passport contains a three-dimensional view of the device, a list of all the materials and components, including weight specifications, as well as specific disassembly instructions for hazardous substances, for materials that could possibly disturb the recycling process and for recyclable/ recoverable materials.[4] The concept facilitates the provision of information on two levels: On the level of anonymous provision of information, it enables the manufacturer to comply with the legally stipulated requirements on information provision by making the information available in the form of recycling passports and thus supplying the recycling company with information that supports them in the material recycling. On a second level, detailed product information is supplied, which supports the decision-making and planning processes within the scope of the co-operation between manufacturers and recycling companies and permits the realisation of higher-grade closed loop strategies such as the re-use of components or products. Over the course of the StreaM project, a prototype was developed and implemented in sample processes within the scope of the case studies. The latest developments in information technology were deployed and the relevant data was first compiled

---

[4] See Dietrich 1999

in a suitable database, which then makes the data available and accessible on the Internet.[5] The information concept, particularly the creation and use of the recycling passport, must be integrated into the internal environment of the manufacturer and the recycling company. To this end, specifications were developed at both Agfa-Gevaert AG and Electrocycling GmbH that outlined the way in which such an integration has to be adjusted due to the company-specific particulars. Based on this, a general procedure for generating and using recycling passports was developed. This is presented in the PAS 1049 (Publicly Available Specification[6]), which was developed in the course of StreaM (PAS 1049 2004). Along with concepts for integrating the task of creating recycling passports at the manufacturer and using the recycling passports in recycling companies, the PAS also contains a detailed description of the structure, contents and format of a recycling passport. In order to avoid a premature discussion of this standardisation approach, implementation options for the StreaM project industrial partners will be focused on here. In particular, the useable information sources as well as the task of creating recycling passports will be examined with respect to Agfa-Gevaert AG, while the discussion on Electrocycling GmbH will concentrate on the use of recycling passports.

7.3.1 Agfa-Gevaert AG Information Sources

At Agfa-Gevaert AG, the central product development database, PEDB, is available as an information source for the product-relevant information required for the recycling passport. In the future, however, information about the complete product life cycle will be represented in an SAP R/3 based Product Life Cycle Management (PLM) module. The pictures of the equipment, which are needed for the graphic images in the recycling passport, can generally be taken from the service documentation or the respective image data from the CAD systems. Agfa-Gevaert AG also uses *Equipment Information Sheets* (EIS), in order to provide customers with a compact version of the relevant environmental data. This information is collected at the same time the recycling passport is created. The compatible and transferable structure of the EIS also allows access to product

---

[5] An in-depth presentation of the StreaM information concept can be found in Spengler and Stölting 2003.

[6] The PAS is a document that contains the technical specifications about a product, process, procedure or service and is publicly available via the Beuth-Verlag publishing house. It fills the gap between consensus-based standardisation and proprietary standardisation.

information about the product components procured from the suppliers and is accordingly used for this task.

7.3.2 Creating Recycling Passports at Agfa-Gevaert AG

At Agfa-Gevaert AG, the task of adjusting and implementing the recycling passport concept is the responsibility of the Corporate Ecodesign department. Among others, departmental tasks include the formulation of corresponding company-internal Ecodesign guidelines and specifications regarding the contents and the tasks needing be performed as well as the preparation of format templates for the recycling passports to be created. The exact guidelines concerning the format, contents, colouring, etc. are specified in a *master recycling passport*. Corporate Ecodesign also prepares pertinent questionnaires, forms such as the equipment information sheet or checklists for querying product information from the suppliers. The actual creation of the recycling passport is then carried out by the competent employee in the project team of the respective development department in the individual business units. This employee applies the guidelines specified in the master recycling passport and can access the information that is compiled in the PEDB product development database by the developers and design engineers. Furthermore, the employee must also obtain any missing information by using the questionnaire, form or checklist templates provided by Corporate Ecodesign for the purpose of querying the supplier. In case of questions regarding content, the employee can consult Corporate Ecodesign at any time. Maintaining and updating the recycling passport is another essential task. This task is assumed by the competent project team employee who is informed about the changes regarding the equipment and can thus monitor the up-to-dateness of the recycling passport. Corporate Ecodesign is in charge of monitoring the updating process as well as the approval and release of the recycling passport. Accordingly, this department also bears the direct responsibility for each published recycling passport.

7.3.3 Use of Recycling Passports at Recycling Companies

The recycling passport is the basis for the calculation and preparation of the tender for taking in charge of the used equipment and its recycling. The following sections present a more detailed description of the use of the recycling passport, as well as the utilisation of the information contained therein, within the scope of the equipment-related case studies conducted in the project.

7.4 Recycling

Since Electrocycling GmbH was not previously familiar with the equipment taken back by Agfa-Gevaert AG, the equipment can be used to analyse the potentials of the developed information and planning tools. The recycling company is provided with an online recycling passport in the course of the recycling planning. During the recycling process, on the basis of optimisation models, an economically efficient disassembly operation takes place,[7] ending with the processing.

The ADC 70 is characterised by a high metal content. More than 75% of its product components are completely made from metal. The device is comprised of several printed circuit boards, motors, transformers, and a number of electronic assemblies. In terms of material recycling, it is thus a relatively valuable piece of equipment. In this regard, the following potentials arise for recycling companies:

- usage of the product information in the recycling passport to support the company in its calculations and operative planning, and
- usage of the product information in the recycling passport during the disassembly operation.

7.4.1 Calculation

The starting point for the calculation was the ADC 70 recycling passport. The material data of the recycling passport is shown in figure 7.4. Possible disassembly operations were identified for the planning calculations.

---

[7] Detailed information on operational planning for recycling companies can be found in Spengler et al. 2003.

4.   Recycling Data of ADC 70, Type 5140

Recycling/Material code	weight approx. (kg)	Important information
Material/components, which must be removed and treated separately		
Lithium battery	0.04	On VME rack and right side panel on RK 188
Electrolytic capacitors (possibly with PCB)	0.68	Part of power electronics
subtotal	**0.72**	
Material/components, which can disturb certain recycling processes		
LCD-Display	0.20	
Oil filling (Klüber: Constand OY 32)	0.39	On friction gear / print module
Attenuates (with oil filling)	1.00	Part of the enclosure
Quartz lamps	0.09	Part of the erase unit
Circuit boards	9.84	Spread over the device
Electric filter unit	1.98	On lower right side panel and part of the activity unit
Complete power supply (circuit boards with capacitors)	1.28	2x part of the activity unit (power supply and laser)
Fiber optic	2.00	Part of the scanner unit, erase unit, print module
Glass, mirrors	1.62	Part of erase unit and print module
>PVC-U<	2.49	Coated with lacquer, in/output buffer
>ABS-FR<	0.50	Housing top / bottom, user terminal
Mixed plastics	3.18	Several small parts, gear, toothed belt, edge protection
Subtotal	**24.57**	
Material/components, through which benefits can be normally be achieved		
Steel, St 1203	170.58	Galvanized, coated with lacquer, complete main chassis, complete enclosures, main board at in/output of cassette unit, setting frame of optic plate, several plates spread over the device
Aluminum (bar stock)	24.14	Bearing chairs, several brackets and all of the rails in the device, several supports, plates and small parts
Aluminum (anodized)	6.41	Several brackets, plate hooks, cooling element in erase unit
Aluminum (sandcasting) (AlSi$_9$Cu$_3$)	1.03	Housing of friction gear in scanner unit
Cast aluminum (AlZnSi$_9$Cu$_3$)	27.29	Optic plate
Stainless steel	24.14	Several axles and shafts, metal sheets at cassette input, back panel erase unit and several hooks
Brass	0.25	Gears and bushes on stepper motor
Mixed metals	15.90	Rollers, several small parts, gears, etc.
>ABS<	0.50	Hopper (enclosure), handle bars, well (optic plate), several lasts
>PVC-U<	0.02	Protection plate input buffer
>PS-HI<	0.63	Funnel mounting rack
>POM<	1.80	Well (enclosure), lift rails, lasts (in/output cassette unit)
Polyurethane foam	0.26	Spread over device
>Si<	0.05	Tubes (sucker)
Motors	2.55	Cassette moving unit top/bottom, scanner unit
Stepper motors	18.48	Spread over the device
Transformers	19.67	Part of the power electronics
Fan	2.58	On mounting rack, (VME rack)
Vacuum pump	0.89	Part of the activity unit
Laser unit	8.00	On optic plate
Several electric components	2.37	Light barriers, support, switches, swinging mirrors, etc.
Cable	13.00	Several cable and cable harness
Subtotal	**340.54**	
composite materials		
Metal / >POM<	0.29	Lasts at cassette input
subtotal	**0.29**	
TOTAL WEIGHT	**366.12**	
Special Notes		
none		

Fig. 7.4. Recycling passport information for ADC 70

In a first step, all product components that have to be removed are defined. On the one hand, these are product components whose removal is legally stipulated. They are located in the first category of the recycling passport as *materials/ components which must be removed and treated separately*. On the other hand, these also include product components whose removal is required in line with the recycling company's technical requirements for the mechanical processing. They are located under further categories in the recycling passport. At Electrocycling GmbH, for example, all electric motors weighing two kg or more and all transformers weighing 20 kg and up are removed, since such compact product components increase the wear-and-tear on the shredder. Product components whose separate sale could possibly bring in higher proceeds as compared to mechanical processing are classified as *potentially profitable product components*. The remaining material/ components have to be summarised under the least possible number of product components, in order to minimise the input data to be considered during the optimisation process. They do not have a separate value as product components in themselves and are not of any interest when determining the disassembly plan. Only their material composition has a value. Under the "composite materials" category, the remaining components are aggregated into product components having the same composition. After identifying the components contained in a device, the locations of the product components within the device have to be determined. Using the disassembly guidelines in the recycling passport, a disassembly diagram is created for the device (see Figure 7.5).

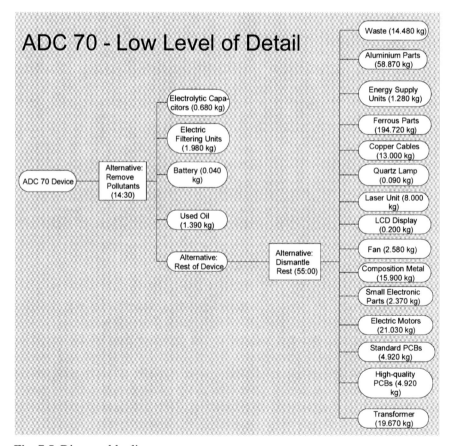

Fig. 7.5. Disassembly diagram

The disassembly times and weights for the materials and components to be disassembled are then assigned to the created disassembly diagrams.

The weights can be taken from the recycling passport. The disassembly times have to be estimated in accordance with the projected disassembly step, based on the information and the experience of the employee performing the calculation. The times and weights are the basis of the monetary assessment. A cost unit rate of 30 € per working hour is estimated for the working time. The first disassembly operation describes all obligatory disassemblies, the second disassembly operation describes the dismantling and removal of all potentially profitable product components. The time for the first operation corresponds to the time for all obligatory disassembly operations. The time for the second operation corresponds to the times for all further disassembly operations. In the planning calculations solution, both operations are performed. The disassembly time was calculated at 69.5 minutes. The minimum pick-up price to be obtained was determined to be -42.6 € per piece/ -116 € per ton.

In conjunction with the recycling passport as a starting basis, the determination of the disassembly depth using the optimisation model provided a more accurate calculation than the Acquisition department employees, who evaluated the device based on their experience or made a rough estimate on the basis of the recycling passport, without deriving the disassembly operations, taking into account the disassembly costs and determining the optimal disassembly depth. Nevertheless, the employees were sceptical about the accuracy of the information in the recycling passports, since they had encountered problems in the past with documents provided by manufacturers.

7.4.2 Disassembly

The disassembly experiments were carried out with full-time Electrocycling GmbH dismantlers at their workplace in Goslar. In addition to observing the experiments, interviews with the dismantlers were conducted for analysis purposes. The dismantlers were questioned about the recycling passport in regards to the following criteria: usefulness in the disassembly process, comprehensibility, suggestions for improvements. The ADC 70 was dismantled in conjunction with the use of a recycling passport. In these cases using recycling passports, the work instructions for the disassembly consisted of markings specifying the product components on the recycling passport. The objective of the empirical study was to examine whether an improvement in the disassembly quality could be determined and whether usage of the recycling passport expedited the disassembly process. The employees worked very closely with the recycling passport. At the beginning of the disassembly process, they used it to attain an overview of the disassembly steps that had to be carried out.

During the actual disassembly operation, the employees repeatedly referred to the recycling passport for control purposes.

At the end of the dismantling job, the document was used to check and verify the disassembly specifications. The employees approved of the general structure of the recycling passport. The individual sections were easy to understand and logically organised. The subsequent interviews made it clear that the employees only utilised the first three sections of the recycling passport, primarily focusing on the drawings. The information mostly went ignored.

In the case of a complex device with many panelling elements on the inside as well, there is a very high risk that pollutants inside the device will be overlooked. It thus has to be assumed that many problematic product components in the ADC 70 would not have been found without the recycling passport. Through the use of the recycling passport, all specified product components were identified and disassembled. In the experiments, the recycling passport therefore ensured a very high level of disassembly quality.

Using the recycling passport for dismantling product components for separate sale turned out to be difficult. First of all, only the standard components, such as motors and transformers, could be removed with the recycling passport. Identified special components, such as a laser unit, could not be disassembled because the dismantler was not familiar with the appearance of the component he was supposed to remove. This led to the conclusion that for the dismantling of special components and specifically selected spare parts, it is absolutely essential to provide pictures of those components/ parts in the recycling passport. To support the targeted disassembly of reusable product components, the dismantlers must have much more information at their disposal in the form of descriptions or training.

In this case study, a reduction in the disassembly time could not be verified due to an insufficient number of test devices. However, the observation of the conducted experiments suggest the supposition that the time savings resulting from lower search efforts are consumed by the time spent for using the recycling passport. Nevertheless, it can be expected that employee experience in handling the recycling passport can reduce the time required.

7.4.3 Results of the Recycling Process

To summarise, the recycling of the ADC 70 yielded the following findings:

- The recycling passport is useful for facilitating decisions pertaining to the planning and calculation.
- Using the recycling passport can prevent pollutants and detrimental substances from being "overlooked", thus improving the quality of the disassembly, especially in terms of the environmental impact.
- In some cases, the time saved during dismantling does not compensate the time spent searching in documents.
- Recycling passports are practical for capital and industrial goods, since, due to the complexity of these devices, the quality of the disassembly could be significantly improved through the use of the information provided in the passport.
- If the intent is to re-use product components, the information in the recycling passport often does not suffice. In this case, more detailed dismantling instructions are needed. In this regard, however, the service documents are also unsuitable, since they contain far too much information for the employees. Accordingly, the re-use of product components from the ADC 70 is examined in the following section.

7.5 Re-use of Product Components from ADC 70

The aim is to re-use the product components from the ADC 70 as spare parts. For this, it was necessary to inspect and evaluate the devices in advance. In co-ordination with the development department and spare parts planners at Agfa-Gevaert AG, after conducting a visual inspection of the ADC 70 unit that had been taken back, a list was prepared containing the relevant modules, assemblies and components that could be used as spare parts. This list, the recycling passport and the pertinent service documentation, such as e.g. the spare parts lists (see Figure 7.6.) were then given to Electrocycling GmbH. The experiments conducted at Electro-cycling GmbH were carried out as a disassembly experiment. To this end, two employees disassembled two different ADC 70 devices on two consecutive days. The experiments were differentiated by dissimilar degrees of detail in the information provided for removing the required components.

 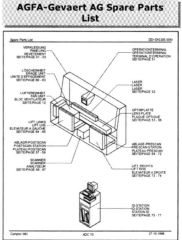

Fig. 7.6. Documents for the recovery of spare parts in the recycling company

For the first experiment, the documents, consisting of the table listing the parts to be recovered, the schematic diagrams, including the main components, and exploded views were provided. In addition, the parts to be recovered were highlighted in colour in both the schematic diagrams and the exploded views. In comparison to the first experiment, considerably fewer exploded views were provided in the second experiment. A corresponding picture was only included if the parts requiring recovery were not a part of the main assemblies that were visible on the schematic diagram. Furthermore, information about the initial access to the device and about the panels to be disassembled was also supplied, so that the findings of the first experiment could already be used to improve the processes.

In contrast to the disassembly experiment that focused on the utilisation of the standard recycling passport, in which the main objective was to analyse the usefulness of the recycling passport in regards to the identification and disassembly of the materials requiring separate treatment, this series of experiments concentrated on non-destructive disassembly. The objective here was the efficient and thus qualitatively high-grade dismantling and removal of the parts to be recovered, including the final professional packaging and transport to Agfa-Gevaert AG. Extensive quality inspections could not be conducted, only visual inspections of obvious damage were performed.

Since the employees at Electrocycling GmbH were not familiar with the devices, the provided documents and specifications were of great significance. Due to the necessity of a non-destructive dismantling process, the parts to be recovered and the associated main assemblies first had to be identified and inspected, for the purpose of preventing any inadvertently caused damage during the disassembly (see Figure 7.7.).

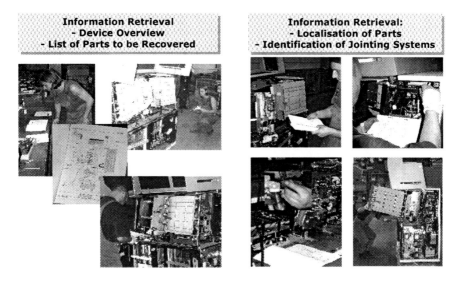

Fig. 7.7. Identification of parts by means of the provided documentation

The unique identification of the targeted parts was made possible by barcodes and printed drawing numbers affixed to both the main assemblies and the printed circuit boards. The problem here was that the stickers are not always visible during the initial access, and thus the parts could only be identified after the disassembly. Since the ADC 70 is a technically very complex device, comprised of many separately distributed electronic assemblies and extensive wiring, the amount of time required for identifying the main assemblies, the position of the targeted parts and for understanding and recognising the assemblies in relation to the actual disassembly and removal process is relatively high (see Figure 7.8.).

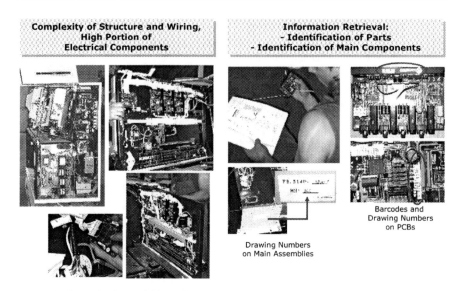

Fig. 7.8. Complexity and identification options

The tools required for the disassembly are shown in figure 7.9. Despite the objective of performing a non-destructive disassembly, a hammer and chisel were needed to remove the ADC 70's scanner unit, since otherwise the device would have necessitated a far more complex removal operation. Destroying a fixture reduced disassembly time, without damaging the main assembly. Specific special-purpose tools were not required for these experiments. In other cases, information in the document might prove helpful, as the respective tool(s) could be provided in advance.

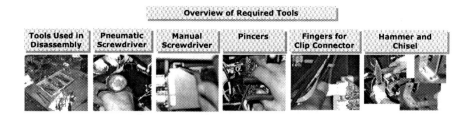

Fig. 7.9. Tools used in the disassembly

By way of example, the removal of the scanner unit and the recovery of a printed circuit board from the scanner unit will be described in the following (see Figure 7.10.). The scanner unit is located in the lower half and is the largest assembly in the device. Due to its weight, two employees were needed to remove the unit and an electric forklift truck was deployed to lift the scanner unit onto a europallet and place it at an ergonomic working height. After the targeted parts had been removed, de-dusted and partially cleaned, they were packed into their respective packaging units, labelled (drawing number, removal data, device serial number) and prepared for shipping. In this context, it was determined that it would be helpful if packaging instructions were provided in the documents, particularly if there are any special conditions in regards to handling and storage. The parts were then shipped to Agfa-Gevaert AG.

Fig. 7.10. Recovering the GS adapter plate from the ADC 70's scanner unit

During the dismantling, the documents provided were heavily used and significantly contributed to the success. The employees rated the documents as being helpful in removing the components. In some cases, the exploded views contained in the recycling passport were perceived as being confusing. The jointing systems and interdependencies were examined on the product itself rather than by consulting the exploded views. For the purpose of standardising the structural data pertaining to the device, an expanded recycling passport thus suggests itself as a medium for transferring information from the manufacturer to the recycling company. For this reason, an initial approach for transferring information for spare parts recovery was developed on the basis of the field experiments, as is illustrated in figures 7.11., 7.12. and 7.13. Options for improving the provision of information particularly lie in the

- provision of information regarding the initial access to the device;
- information indicating whether the components have to be removed together with the corresponding wires;
- instructions regarding the procedure for dismantling assembled units for which a need exists; and
- improvements in the schematic diagrams in terms of clarifying which part has to be removed.

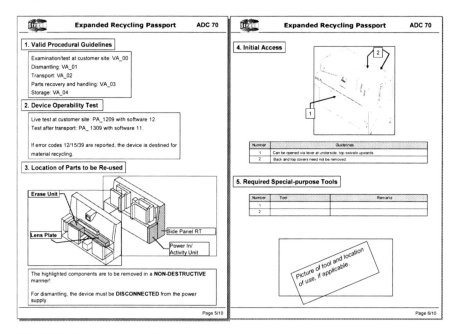

Fig. 7.11. Expanded recycling passport for spare parts recovery (1)

In principle, for the transfer of information between the manufacturer and the recycling company, with respect to recovering spare parts from used devices, a determination should be made as to whether product information (device purpose and type of device, position of spare parts, identification of parts), process information (disassembly, handling, storage and transport guidelines) or dynamic job information (deinstallation/ collection, deadline/ schedule, specific customer data, etc.) should be transferred.

A special emphasis was therefore placed on the conceptualisation of an expanded recycling passport containing the necessary information for a spare parts recovery process, thus enabling the dismantler to properly disassemble the device and recover the targeted parts. The expanded recycling passport can be seen as an extension of the *normal* recycling passport, which already contains information about dimensions and weight as well as an identification of the device type.

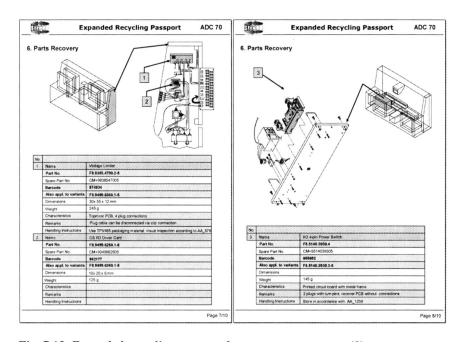

Fig. 7.12. Expanded recycling passport for spare parts recovery (2)

Since the spare parts recovery operation takes place within the framework of a co-operative relationship between manufacturer and recycling company, the underlying service level agreement also defines the structure of the expanded recycling passport. The following aspects need to be considered:

- Procedural guidelines: Within the scope of co-operations with suppliers, the specifications to be implemented by the supplier are documented in the form of performance specifications. This also takes place in the extended supply chain, in order to facilitate development of the procedural and work instructions for handling the devices needing dismantling. The specifications provide the basis for the activities to be carried out, with the device-specific information contained in the expanded recycling passport.

- Testing: it is supposed that a test of the device's operability and determination of the error codes are relevant for further processing, in order to be able to establish a performance based classification into "Used/Reconditioned" in accordance with DIN Draft 48480. For this testing, the recycling company has to be provided with the same pertinent testing software that is deployed by the service technician. Furthermore, there is also the option of deciding, even before the dismantling operation, which re-use/ recycling path should be pursued. It is therefore conceivable, e.g., that certain error codes indicate that spare parts recovery is no longer feasible and a recycling operation should be carried out. Such testing options should already be allowed for during the development of the software.

- Position of parts: identification and labelling of the approximate position of the parts to be recovered is important, in case the device has to be partially destroyed. The main assemblies containing the targeted parts should be dismantled in a non-destructive manner.

- Initial access: the disassembly experiments demonstrated that information and instructions regarding the initial access and opening of the device prove very useful. Information about the panels that do not require dismantling can positively affect the disassembly time.

- Special-purpose tools: special-purpose auxiliary devices or tools, such as, e.g., rather rarely used, company-specific torx screwdrivers, etc., which can facilitate the disassembly process, may be needed for a non-destructive dismantling operation. These special-purpose tools are, for example, also listed in the spare parts list in the form of notes and provide valuable information in regards to reducing the disassembly time, since such tools can be provided for within the course of the work preparations.

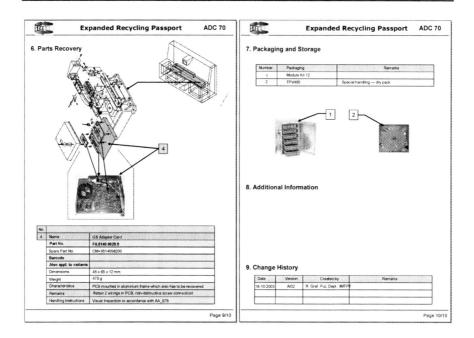

Fig 7.13. Expanded recycling passport for spare parts recovery (3)

- Parts identification: the basis of the spare parts recovery is the identification. Visual illustrations and schematic diagrams or exploded views are used for this. The parts to be recovered are labelled with a number in the identification documents and additional information is provided in tabular form, as is the case with the *regular* recycling passport. At Agfa-Gevaert AG, the most important information includes the parts number and the barcode, which are affixed to the parts. Moreover, the spare parts number is relevant for comparison with the service documents and for the return, or in the case that a spare part has already been assembled there. The disassembly experiments also showed that information about specific characteristics can also be very helpful in more quickly narrowing down the identification from among the multitude of mounted components and only then performing a number comparison. Examples of this are illustrated in figures 7.12. and 7.13. Moreover, it is important to provide, e.g., any information about any special packaging types that are not covered by the agreed-upon standard procedural instructions.
- Packaging and storage: in this area, additional handling information is provided.

- Additional information: this field is used to provide useful information regarding the handling, disassembly and recovery of the parts.

Since an *expanded recycling passport* can also be subject to changes over the course of time, a history section for tracking changes should also be included. Options here include providing the *expanded recycling passport* on a per disassembly job basis or downloading it via the communication platform in order to ensure access to the most recent version.

Along with the disassembly studies, the printed circuit boards were also analysed with respect to their components and remaining supply periods. The delivery information was examined at www.totalparts.com and figure 7.14. shows a selection of the printed circuit boards.

It became apparent that at the end of the supply period, most of the components on the analysed printer circuit boards that could be identified and thus examined (approx. 15%) had already been discontinued or were to be discontinued within 12 months. As a result, post-production, as is usually carried out at Agfa-Gevaert AG in the event of supply bottlenecks, is no longer possible. For this reason, the re-use of components from used equipment can be an alternative procurement source.

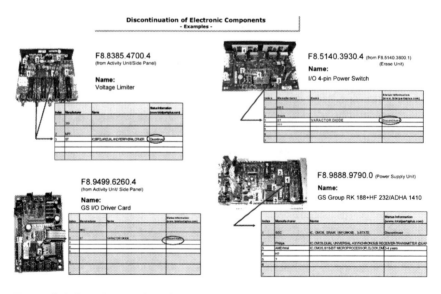

Fig. 7.14. Selected examples of component discontinuation

In the voltage limiter example, the planned (projected) demands and remaining demands as well as the remaining stock were analysed at Agfa-Gevaert AG, as figure 7.47. shows. It was determined that, according to the 1997 forecast, the corresponding spare part had a remaining demand of

37 parts, but only 25 parts were available. The extrapolation of the forecast using 6 years of updated history and consumption data allows an expected reduction from 12 to 6 missing parts up until the end of the supply. From the returns of the ADC 70, on the other hand, three of the printed circuit boards could be recovered, which were tested at Agfa-Gevaert AG. While the remaining service life could not be accurately determined, the printed circuit boards were generally operational and if needed, could be used by the respective spare parts planner in Customer Service Organisation as an option for meeting customer requirements, if necessary. Thus, an extensive and costly re-designing of a printed circuit board with a lot size of 6 pieces could be avoided. Still to be resolved is whether the newly forecasted remaining demand corresponds to the actual demand and whether in the case of malfunctions, customers will allow a parts replacement with used product components due to the age of the device. In terms of utilising the recovered spare parts for customer use, an analysis needs to be conducted to determine whether the offer of *used*, *reconditioned* and *new* spare parts will be accepted; such an analysis should be based on the requirements, conceptions, willingness to pay and risk considerations on the part of the respective customer.[8]

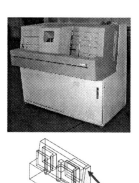
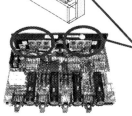

ADC 70 (as of mid-2003) Sample Device

- End of Supply Period: 12/2004
- "Voltage Limiter" Spare Part Availability
  - "Remaining demand" forecast
    (as of 1997): **37 parts.**
  - In stock: **25 parts.**
  - Actual planned demand
    (new forecast 2003): **31 parts.**
- Component analyses showed that 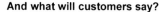 - 6
  - ICs for PCBs are no longer available,
  - re-manufacturing is not possible, and
  - remaining stock is insufficient.

And what will customers say?

"Voltage Limiter Unit" PCB	**Status**
Manufacturer: ST	**Information**
Name: IC, Bipolar, Dual and	
Peripheral Driver	**(www.totalparts**
Status: **Discontinued**	**plus.com)**

Fig. 7.15. Example of supply gap due to component discontinuance

---

[8] For more on this classification, also see (DIN 48480 2000).

A case study on spare parts supplying through the re-use of product components from used equipment was also carried out in the StreaM project. The following section discusses the concept developed for redesigning the manufacturer's business processes, which is necessary for implementing such a strategy.

7.6 Spare Parts Supplying at Agfa-Gevaert AG, Using ADC Compact Example

Agfa-Gevaert AG is organisationally divided into three business units, to which the staff departments and decentralised production plants are assigned. The regional sales organisations are independent companies that undertake the co-ordination, planning and management of the after-sales activities via a customer care center. Spare parts provision is a central task and is ensured by a central warehouse in Munich (see Figure 7.16). The orders for spare parts from the technical customer service departments, sales organisations and end customers who perform in-house maintenance are received at the warehouse. In the central warehouse based in Munich, approx. 27,000 items are managed and stored, covering approx. 40% of the worldwide spare parts demand. From a total stock volume of approx. 55 million euro, about 30-40% are attributable to end-of-life stock. In addition, the trend in producing digital equipment is reflected in the inventory value, since as a rule, the spare parts are assessed at increasingly higher values. As a result of the rising capital tie-up costs and the component discontinuance on the part of the semiconductor industry, alternatives for supplying spare parts, apart from end-of-life stockkeeping, are becoming more and more relevant.

When determining the spare parts and demand, it should be kept in mind that a basic supply is guaranteed upon the first delivery of the device. The decision concerning which parts shall be declared spare parts is jointly made by Development, Production, the central departments of the business unit, the technical centre and Customer Support, as early as during the development phase. Key factors that play a role in the process of determining spare parts include, among others, the service life of the device, options for disassembly, wear characteristics, shelf life as well as the consumption history of the predecessor model. Furthermore, the necessary quality inspections are specified and the production costs are determined. On this basis, an economically efficient lot size for manu-facturing the spare part(s) is then established and registered.

**European Central Warehouse
in Munich, Germany**

- Delivery performance: 95%, target >98%.
- Storage for approx. 40% of international spare parts demand.
- Stock: approx. 70,000 parts for approx. 27,000 items.
- Inventory value: approx. 55 million €.
- Daily inventory movements: approx. 1800 parts.
- Contractual delivery times: 3 hrs. / 24 hrs. / 48 hrs. within Europe.
- Approx. 40% of inventory serves to meet end-of-life stockkeeping.

Fig. 7.16. Key indices of the central spare parts warehouse

During the *series production phase*, the lot size is stochastically calculated with the assistance of the reorder point, which is supported by an SAP PPS module and the spare parts supply system (SPS). The basis for the spare parts demand planning are the currently recorded repair orders from the customer service requests of the national service organisations as well as the forecasted monthly consumption derived from the consumption history values, which are managed in the service management system

The preparations for the spare parts provision of the *after-series production* are generally initiated six months prior to the end of production. For all spare parts that will not be further produced for other product types, the overall demand is determined and the lot size of the final lot for the end-of-life stock is suggested. Among other things, the overall demand depends on the current parts stock in the central warehouse, the buffer stocks of the sales organisations, consumption history, empirical values of the predecessor models and the quantity of primary products offered on the market.

For the purposes of monitoring the stock in the central warehouse, a periodic variance comparison of the stock on hand is conducted for end-of-life spare parts. If insufficiencies arise in the actual stocks, the production equipment that had been stored in the interim is put back into operation and used to manufacture another lot. This *safety backup* option greatly increases production costs as a result of restarting the production equipment and places high demands on storage as well as warehouse capacities and the reactivation of the production know-how. If electronic components are no longer available or have been discontinued, a re-design operation is performed along with all the required quality inspections and any necessary approval procedures. For complex units and functional and signal integration into the BUS systems, the average costs of such a redesign can be calculated at several 100,000 €. Instead of these expensive variants, more cost-effective alternatives can be created by exploiting the re-use options.

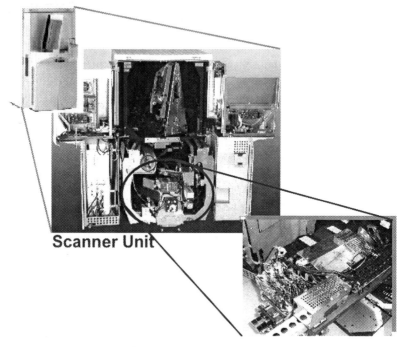

Fig. 7.17. ADC compact and scanner unit

For the ADC Compact, which is being phased out, the scanner unit was identified as one of the most important spare parts (see Figure 7.17.). This large assembly consists of a lens unit and a scanner unit. The lens unit consists of a galvanometer, photomultiplier and a He-Ne laser; the scanner unit comprises prescan and postscan stations with transport rollers and coupling elements as well as fibre optics. The laser beam for scanning and exposing the imaging plates is guided via several flip mirrors, which are internally regulated by a gear control unit. Thus, the adjustment of the interplay between the laser and laser beam guidance in combination with the photomultiplier and the galvanometer is a highly complex, sophisticated and quality-indicating feature of the ADC device types and is a task which can only be performed with the use of special equipment. A demand of approx. 472 pieces over a period of seven years was forecasted for the after-series production of the scanner unit. Figure 7.18. shows the result of applying a decision tree method for determining a supply strategy that not only takes into account the end-of-life stock, but also alternative supply approaches.

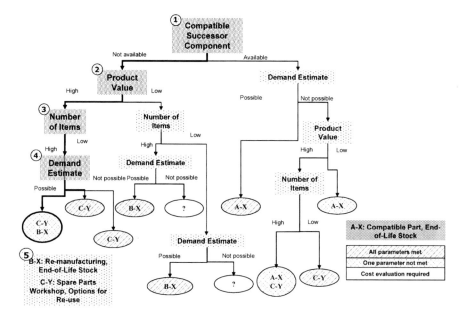

Fig 7.18. Decision tree method for determining the supply strategy for the ADC compact scanner unit

The successor product, the ADC Compact Plus, comprises only about 50% of the same parts. Since the successor product guarantees increased efficiency and performance with regard to productivity and speed (imaging plate output), the new requirements necessitate the use of new printed circuit boards, improved components, higher-performance photomultipliers and lasers. Therefore, malfunctioning parts are not compatible with the new parts (1). The value of the scanner unit (2), compared with the total value of the product, amounts to 70% (high) and the required and forecasted demand also has to be classified as high (3). Since the failures of the scanner unit, including the laser unit, galvanometer, storage of the flip mirrors, etc., are 97% due to wear and the sporadic failure rate of the electronic components amounts to approx. 3%, a demand estimate can be easily calculated (4). The theoretical supply strategies resulting from the decision tree must be checked for consistency in the next step. Post-production is not an option for the scanner unit, since the equipment, tools and other facilities are being modified for the production of the ADC

Compact Plus successor product. Thus, outsourcing the post-production to an external partner is also not an alternative, particularly as the scanner unit requires specialised technical expertise that should not be made available to third parties. Due to the number of pieces over the supply period in proportion to the series production, minor learning curve effects are to be expected. The associated costs and investments for providing the equipment and resources are thus not at all proportionate. On account of the expected high investments, new or reproductions of the equipment and resources are also ruled out.

Therefore, the *supply approach* of a final lot for end-of-life stock-keeping in combination with re-use options represents a possible and feasible alternative. These options can particularly be used to cover forecast uncertainties near the end of the supply period. The emergency option of a redesign can always be applied, however, it also represents the most expensive variant of the supply approaches.

Due to the application in the medicine-technical sector and the high value of the product, the customer needs to be provided with used spare parts in "good-as-new" (i.e. reconditioned) quality. To this end, all the wearing parts of the scanner are replaced, thus limiting the re-use options to remanufacturing. Since the scanner unit is a technically high-grade and complex spare part, the quality of the imaging plate processing depends on the adjustment of the laser mimics, and specific equipment and testing systems are required, only Agfa-Gevaert AG itself can carry out the remanufacturing process.

Due to the required know-how, it is logical that the production facility is entrusted with this task. At the same time, it is important for this scanner unit that a *defective* part is replaced by a *reconditioned* or *new* part. On the one hand, the repair time is not at the expense of the customer and a high availability is achieved, on the other hand, the Service department does not have the necessary equipment for fine tuning in the case of extensive repair work. This leads to a *supply strategy* comprising end-of-life stockkeeping and subsequent remanufacturing with an active take-back strategy on the part of the sales and service organisations. The remanufacturing process is carried out by the production facility. In the following, the new business processes required on the part of the manufacturer for the purpose of implementing the selected supply strategy is conceptually designed (Herrmann et al. 2004).

The *implementation of the supply strategy* depends on the IT (information technology) support via the spare parts warehouse, where the defective scanner units also accumulate from the field and from there can be requisitioned by the production facility for remanufacturing. At Agfa-Gevaert AG, a *warehouse information system* is deployed for the warehouse management of spare parts, which in addition to its function as a spare parts supply system (SPS), is also used as a parts supply system. The system consists of various subsystems for meeting these tasks. Along with the internal system interfaces, there are also external interfaces, via which six different systems are linked. The internal relationships are shaped by the central function of the inventory management subsystem, which offers basic warehouse management functions. Due to its planning functions, the functionality of the system suggests parallels to PPS systems in some areas. The provided functions for demand planning, stock planning and the option for making decisions in regards to procuring required goods/ meeting existing demand have both a planning and controlling character. Moreover, the system is supplemented with the SAP AG PPS system. The order co-ordination process is triggered by a purchasing requisition from the spare parts warehouse. The option of including used parts in the purchasing requisition necessitates a description of the perfromance characteristics and age, along with the product description and the required quantity. In addition to skipping process steps such as request evaluation and tender preparation (Luczak et al. 1998), process expansions are also necessary. Figure 7.19. shows the order broken down into up to three suborders in accordance with the conditions of the parts: *Used Part*, *Reconditioned Part* and *New Part*. In addition to the bills of material generated via the master data, the parts have to be assigned to the corresponding procurement sources. Based on the characteristics of the procurement sources and after assigning the parts to them, feedback regarding the order status and estimated delivery to the spare parts warehouse can be provided. The subsequent process steps comprise the classification of the suborders into the processing step categories, for which specific orders are generated.

In the case of internal further processing based on internal procurement, in a periodic serial production, the same process steps are executed as in the existing PPS systems. If the decision is made for a final lot, the existing manual process for determining total use is initiated, its results entered into the PPS system and accordingly scheduled, planned and controlled. In case of external procurement and internal processing, a process for ordering used parts is initiated with an order calculation. The same process is initiated for external processing, the difference being that the order is subdivided according to the respective order categories at the beginning of the order procedure. Consequently, the order proposal is checked in both cases and the order is released. A delivery order is triggered, monitored until the incoming goods are received and then posted, as shown in figure 7.20.

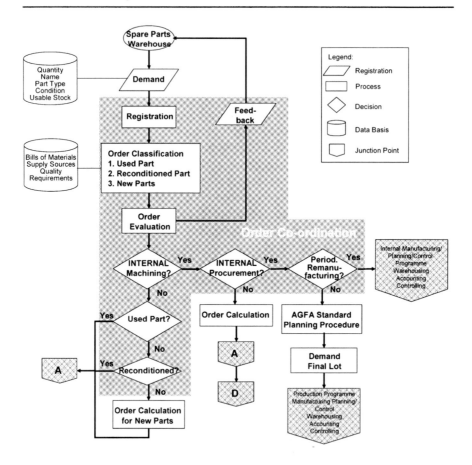

Fig. 7.19. Order co-ordination

In the case of external processing, the incoming parts are stored in the spare parts warehouse after the completion of the external procurement planning and controlling process. In the section dealing with the receipt of the parts, disposal management is mentioned in addition to the accounting. Since the parts have been externally processed and thus also tested, sorting them via a disposal management system is not necessary. In the event of qualitatively insufficient goods, a gradation of the product's performance level and the appropriate storage for later sale or a return to the external manufacturer would still be an option.

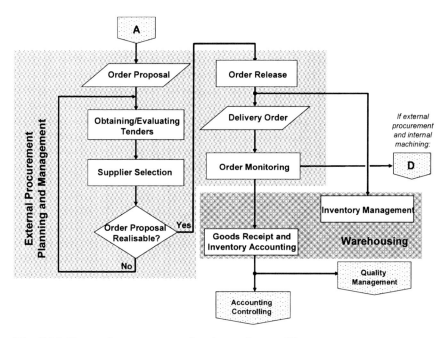

Fig. 7.20. External procurement planning and controlling

In the case of internal processing and external procurement, upon completion of the external procurement and controlling process, the incoming parts are registered and non-useable parts are disposed of. In accordance with the quality of the parts and the demand situation, the subsequent order co-ordination generates the orders for further processing in the course of upgrade, remanufacturing or repair jobs or, if parts are allocated for re-use, an order for direct storage in the spare parts warehouse (see Figure 7.21.). Following that, the quality data is recorded and the parts are stored in the spare parts warehouse.

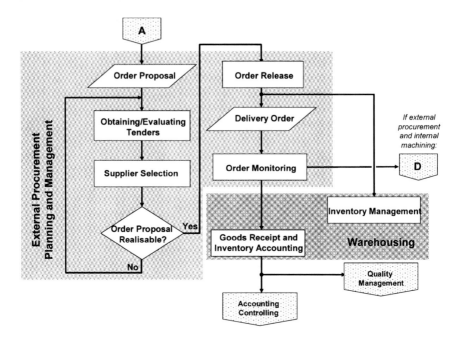

Fig. 7.21. Order classification and assignment

The processes described here constitute a system that is triggered by a reorder point procedure for a stochastic lot size calculation in the spare parts warehouse, as is the case at Agfa-Gevaert AG. Integrated planning for the spare parts warehouse and the processes presented here would be possible and would only require minor expansions. With this combination, it must be noted that in the warehouse, items do not only have to be differentiated by product identification but also by age and performance characteristics. Accordingly, it was ensured in the processes shown here that all supply approaches and order processing activities could be performed in parallel, successively, and individually.

After the re-use options had been integrated into the existing spare parts order co-ordination at Agfa-Gevaert AG, the planning and control processes for the internal re-use orders were developed. To this end, the planning systems at Agfa-Gevaert AG are taken as a basis and supplies are provided via the central warehouse for spare parts by means of kanban control. This enables company-internal implementation via a re-use centre or through integration into the existing serial and production processes.

Furthermore, an integrated spare parts management system has interfaces to the technical service, which performs the actual maintenance of the primary products. Since the technical service generally services the product within the scope of maintenance agreements, it can provide both an assessment of the potential re-use as well as define requirements for the use of spare parts from recovery processes. This supplementary information, in combination with maintenance plans, is taken into consideration within the scope of advance planning for the spare parts supply. This enables efficient demand planning for *right* spare parts in regards to quality and requirements, e.g. in terms of appropriate ad valorem repairs, and corresponding re-use orders can be generated.

7.7 Outlook: Strategic Planning for Integrating Product Component Re-use

In the previous section, alternative spare parts strategies for the ADC Compact scanner unit were identified. The following questions need to be analysed within the course of strategic planning:

- What is the value of the enhanced flexibility of the re-use options in regards to ensuring the spare parts supply?
- How should the core processes of the spare parts production, the return and dismantling of used devices as well as the remanufacturing of the product components to be recovered be designed and managed?
- With respect to the design and management of the extended supply chain, what starting points are there for increasing the number of recovered and re-used product components?

In the case of the various strategies examined here, it is apparent that flexible (due to the options for actions depending on the course of events) and robust strategies (a deviation from the forecasted assumptions does not have serious consequences) for supplying spare parts can result in real added value for the companies that deploy them. The integration of product component re-use for supplying spare parts in post-production enables a wide range of innovative design options. An assessment can be conducted on the basis of the planning tools developed in the StreaM project.[9]

---

[9] For a comprehensive description of the StreaM approach for strategic spare parts management planning utilising concepts for re-using product components, please refer to Spengler and Schröter 2003.

7.8 Summary

The creation of closed supply chains is increasingly becoming an essential challenge for companies in the electronics industry. On the one hand, manufacturers worldwide are assuming more and more expanded product stewardship for their equipment as a result of new laws and directives. On the other hand, the formation of substance flow oriented supply chains offers a range of opportunities for enterprises, including the establishment of a *green image* and the exploitation of new market segments. Furthermore, recovery systems offer manufacturers additional procurement sources of materials and product components, e.g. for spare parts management. Accordingly, the objective of the BMBF funded research project *StreaM – Substance Flow Oriented Closed Loop Supply Chain Management in the Electrical and Electronic Equipment Industry* was the provision of strategic and operational planning tools for a substance flow oriented and cross-utilisation phase, boundary independent supply chain management in the electronic industry via the proper further development of existing information systems. The concepts and methods developed in the project were applied within the scope of extensive case studies on-site at the Agfa-Gevaert AG and Electrocycling GmbH industrial partners and the results presented in this paper. In this context, approaches were developed as to how the designed information concept can be implemeted into the corporate environment of these stakeholders. The focus here was the development of a company-independent procedure for creating and using recycling passports, which is published by the *Deutsches Institut für Normung e.V* (German Institute for Standardisation) in the form of a PAS (Publicly Available Specifications). The benefits of the operative planning tool for recycling companies were illustrated by means of a recycling and recovery planning process for a sample used medical-technical device produced by Agfa-Gevaert AG (ADC 70). It could be demonstrated that deployment of the planning tool in conjunction with the use of the recycling passport as data input (i.e. as a means of providing information) enables a more accurate calculation in regards to the device recycling and the recovery of its components. Closure of material supply loops was made possible by the re-use of product components as spare parts. Within the scope of the dismantling experiments at Electrocycling GmbH, the product components targeted by Agfa-Gevaert AG were able to be recovered for the ADC 70 sample device. As a result of the analysis, an expanded recycling passport was developed to facilitate the recovery of spare parts. The implementation of the business processes developed in the project for the integrated planning of spare parts management and recycling were presented using the example of the order co-ordination process.

References

Dietrich K-H (1999) Recyclinggerechte Produktgestaltung im Unternehmen Agfa-Gevaert AG. In: VDI Berichte 1479: Ganzheitliches Recycling Elektr(on)ischer Produkte. VDI-Verlag, Düsseldorf

DIN 48480 (2000) DIN 48480-Entwurf: Elektrotechnik: Gebrauchstauglichkeit und Qualität bei erneuter Verwendung von Teilen und Geräten – Anforderungen und Prüfungen. Beuth, Berlin

EC directive 2002/96/EC (2003) Directive 2002/96/EC of the European Parliament and of the Council of 27 January 2003 on waste electrical and electronic equipment (WEEE). Official Journal of the European Union, 13/02/03

Gungor A, Gupta S-M (1999) Issues in environmentally conscious manufacturing and product recovery: a survey. Computers & Industrial Engineering no 36, pp 811-853

Herrmann C, Graf R, Luger T, Kuhn V (2004) Re-X Options in Closed-Loop Supply Chains for Spare Part Management. In: Proceedings Global Conference on Sustainable Product Development and Life Cycle Engineering, Berlin, pp 139-142

Luczak H, Eversheim W, Schotten M (1998) Produktionsplanung und -steuerung: Grundlagen, Gestaltung und Konzepte. Springer, Berlin Heidelberg New York

Picot A, Reichwald R, Wigand RT (2003) Die grenzenlose Unternehmung. 5th edn, Gabler, Wiesbaden

PAS 1049 (2004) Publicly Available Specification 1049: Transmission of recycling relevant product information betwween producers and recyclers – The recycling passport. Deutsches Insitut für Normung, Beuth Verlag, Berlin

Spengler T, Ploog M, Schröter M (2003) Integrated Planning of Acquisition, Disassembly and Bulk Recycling: A Case Study on Electronic Scrap Recycling. OR Spectrum no 25, pp 413-442

Spengler T, Schröter M (2003) Strategic Management of Spare Parts in Closed-loop Supply Chains – a System Dynamics Approach. Interfaces, Special Issue on Closed-Loop Supply Chain Management no 6, pp 7 – 17

Spengler T, Stölting W (2003) Recycling-Oriented Information Management in Closed Loop Supply Chains in the Electrical and Electronic Equipment Industry. In: Seuring S, Müller M, Goldbach M, Schneidewind U (eds) Strategy and Organization in Supply Chains. Physica, Heidelberg New York, pp. 353-368

8 Developments in Material Flow Management: Outlook and Perspectives

Bernd Wagner, Stefan Enzler

Bernd Wagner, Centre for Further Training and Knowledge Transfer, University of Augsburg, Germany
Email: bernd.wagner@zww.uni-augsburg.de

Stefan Enzler, imu augsburg GmbH & Co.KG, Augsburg/ Germany
Email: enzler@imu-augsburg.de

Material flow management offers enterprises numerous advantages and success potentials. However, practical implementation of this approach is still a slow-going process. There are still a number of obstacles impeding a broader utilisation and application of material flow management. In terms of overcoming these hindrances, further developments are already foreseeable which speak in favour of a successful dissemination of this approach. In order to depict a development path for material flow management, existing obstacles and pending developments are summarised in the following.

8.1 Existing Obstacles to Material Flow Management

There are several obstacles blocking the widespread dissemination of material flow management in corporate practice. The following points demonstrate the necessity for further development of material flow management:

- Already existing value-added chain structures influence stakeholder actions, which in turn affect these structures. This reciprocal interaction significantly restricts the objective-oriented design options of the individual stakeholders. Efficient material flow management requires co-operation on the part of all stakeholders.

- In the scientific and academic discussion, material flow management is often equated with co-operation, based on the simplified concept that companies want to co-operate in a cross-level optimisation of material flows in regards to sustainability. It must be noted, however, that enterprises do not enter into co-operations on a cross-company level unless there are company-specific reasons to do so. Enterprises are market participants and thus natural competitors which, in the absence of political pressure or expected benefits for themselve, do not co-operate for the purpose of designing ecologically sounder material flows.
- The interaction of several organisations requires management. Material flow management offers the impression that the stakeholders are reciprocally managed. However, there is not one sole material flow manager, but rather a co-operation of several organisationally independent managers who aim at optimising their own benefits. The lack of cross value-added chain management for optimising the benefits for all involved parties prevents companies from positively opening up to material flow management.
- On their own, single enterprises are unable to meet the requirements of a sustainable material flow management, i.e. simultaneously managing economic, ecological and social objectives.
- Some material flow management approaches have yet to be tested in practice. The formulated objectives and criteria specify strict requirements which are viewed as mandatory. The practical application of these approaches gives rise to information and co-ordination problems between stakeholders as well as on an individual company level.
- Material flow management is sometimes seen as a separate company task. To attain better acceptance of this promising approach, material flow management has to be more comprehensively integrated into company processes.
- Examining physical material flows alone is not sufficient for reaching an efficient co-operation between several stakeholders. By not taking organisation and information flows into account, co-operation options are only utilised to a limited extent in corporate practice.

8.2 Required Developments in Material Flow Management

The results of the presented research projects as well as the shared conclusions arising from the meetings of the "Material Flow Management and Recovery Systems" working group aim to eliminate existing obstacles preventing the application of material flow management and identify areas that still require research and development in this field. Based on the recent findings, the following development areas can be summarised:

- Standardised data collection and evaluation with ERP system interface
- Industry-specific solutions
- Supplementation of supply chain (value-added chain) evaluations with information flow analyses
- Business models for a culture of innovation
- Dissemination and networking of research results.

8.2.1 Standardised Data Collection and Evaluation with ERP System Interface

To be efficient in the long term, cross-company material flow tracking requires a systematic supply of data. Based on the existing project and institute specific solutions, a standardised solution for securing data collection, availability and quality needs to be developed. A combination of the various findings promises successful further development of already implemented data evaluation methods and, for corporate practice, provides a better overview of the available problem solution approaches and methods.

The method to be standardised must enable simultaneous tracking of material flow quantities/volumes, values and costs and, depending on the company size, provide an interface – as direct as possible – to existing ERP systems. An integrated consideration of ecological, economic and social aspects should be further developed and secured.

8.2.2 Industry-specific Solutions

An integrated data supply should be provided along both the physical value-added chain as well as the product realisation path (from the product concept to design up to realisation). When further developing material flow management approaches, the competitive situation has to be taken into account as well, particularly in regards to a global perspective in the case of cross-border material flows. As a result of competitive pressure, industry consolidation and transparent markets, standards and open forms of co-operation already exist in some industries, while others still urgently require industry-specific solutions, success examples and intensified research and analyses in order to gain better access to the possibilities and opportunities offered by material flow management.

8.2.3 Supplementation of Supply Chain (Value-added Chains) Evaluations with Information Flow Analyses

For the most part, material flow management approaches up to now have examined the physical layer (material and substance flows) in great detail, while only partially taking into account the corresponding internal and cross-company information flows and organisational structures. Information flows control and map the material flows, thus forming the key to more efficiently designing value-added chains. They shape the perceptive and problem awareness of the decision-makers. A special future potential is detected in the optimisation of information flows and organisational structures that correspond to the actual material flows. Here, increased transparency and the resultant design tools can contribute to improving the exchange of information between stakeholders and thus the efficiency of the value-added chain.

8.2.4 Internal Business Models for a Culture of Innovation

Scepticism towards new scientific developments and innovations can often be found in corporate practice. Enterprises could utilise many of the available material flow research results for economic, ecological and social improvements. However, companies are either unfamiliar with these results or reject them. To extensively disseminate these efficient approaches in enterprises, attention thus needs to be focused on the question of which internal business models are required in companies in order to facilitate the acceptance of new management approaches. What information and communication processes, which organisational process and structure models can facilitate efficient, innovative material flow design in companies? Which elements of corporate culture and what competencies are required for employees and managers? Only a refurbishment of existing, traditional business models can trigger new innovation impetuses in corporate practice and thus increase the implementation probability of new approaches and methods.

8.2.5 Dissemination and Networking of Research Results

Research results should provide input for corporate practice, which requires numerous dissemination activities for getting the results to the decision-makers in the companies. More punch is added by networking and harmonising the research results in order to prevent a confusion of tongues and a maze of terminology and ensure that innovative companies are not put off by the multitude of similar approaches and tools. Therefore, research funding should proactively allow for and explicitly demand, to a greater extent, the dissemination of research results beyond the scope of the companies participating in the projects, both on a domestic and international level. The same applies to the exchange, mutual co-ordination and further content development of material flow related research projects.

8.3 Summary

On the whole, the material flow oriented projects within the scope of the "Material Flow Management and Recovery Systems" working group demonstrate a high potential for sustainable developments, i.e., new paths that lead to economic competitive advantages and are also ecologically and socially sound in the long-term. In this context, a series of tools was tested in practice and scientifically further developed. Those material flow management concepts that are based on "classic" tools such as input-output balances or performance indicator systems, but which at the same time enable integrated processing of all material flow data across the individual material flow levels by means of conventional ERP systems appear to be particularly promising. With regards to quantities/volumes and costs, the comprehensive transparency of company-internal and cross-company material flows is a key success factor for material flow management. Supplemented with accompanying ecological information, such a data basis can facilitate the optimisation of material flows in a way that leads to actual competitive advantages. In addition to the systematic supply of data on both an internal and cross-company level, material flow management that consistently examines the information flows that are controlling the material flows is another important factor for the future. The tested approaches demonstrate new options and promising methods. However, the real success lies in widespread practical implementation at the company level. Here, a vast number of potentials are still unused.

The path to the future leads from material flow management towards integrated material and information flow management (flow management).

About the Authors

Beucker, Severin
Fraunhofer Institute for Industrial Engineering (IAO), Institute for
Human Factors and Technology Management (IAT)
University of Stuttgart
Nobelstr. 12, 70569 Stuttgart
Germany
Email: severin.beucker@iao.fraunhofer.de
severin.beucker@iat.uni-stuttgart.de

Busch, Timo
Wuppertal Institute for Climate, Environment, Energy, Sustainable
Production and Consumption
Doeppersberg 19, 42103 Wuppertal
Germany
Email: timo.busch@wupperinst.org

Enzler, Stefan, Dr.
imu augsburg GmbH & Co.KG
Gratzmuellerstr. 3, 86150 Augsburg
Germany
Email: enzler@imu-augsburg.de

Graf, René
Institute of Machine Tools and Production Technology, Department of
Production and Life-Cycle-Management.
Technical University of Braunschweig
Langer Kamp 19b, 38106 Braunschweig
Germany
E-Mail: r.graf@tu-bs.de

Günther, Edeltraud, Prof. Dr.
Department of Business Management and Economics
University of Technology Dresden
Münchner Platz 1/3, 01187 Dresden
Germany
E-Mail: bu@mailbox.tu-dresden.de

Herrmann, Christoph, Dr.
Institute of Machine Tools and Production Technology, Department of
Production and Life-Cycle-Management
Technical University of Braunschweig
Langer Kamp 19b, 38106 Braunschweig
Germany
E-Mail: c.herrmann@tu-bs.de

Horstmann, Uwe
Conti Temic Microelectronic GmbH, Nürnberg
Sieboldstr. 19, 90411 Nürnberg
Germany
Email: uwe.horstmann@temic.com

Kaulich, Susann
Department of Business Management and Economics
University of Technology Dresden
Münchner Platz 1/3, 01187 Dresden
Germany
E-Mail: susann.kaulich@mailbox.tu-dresden.de

Kuchenbuch, André
Department of Environmental Management and Controlling
University of Duisburg-Essen,
BehrHella Thermocontrol GmbH, Lippstadt
Hansastrasse 40, 59557 Lippstadt
Germany
E-Mail: a.kuchenbuch@cityweb.de

Lang-Koetz, Claus
Institute for Human Factors and Technology Management (IAT)
University of Stuttgart
Nobelstr. 12, 70569 Stuttgart
Germany
E-mail: claus.lang-koetz@iao.fraunhofer.de

Lange, Christoph, Prof. Dr.
Department of Environmental Management and Controlling
University of Duisburg-Essen
Universitätsstrasse 11, 45117 Essen
Germany
E-Mail: c.lange@uni-essen.de

Loew, Thomas
Institute for Ecological Economy Research, Berlin
Potsdamer Str. 105, 10785 Berlin
Germany
E-Mail: thomas.loew@ioew.de

Müller, Andreas
TOSHIBA Europe GmbH, Regensburg Operations
Leibnizstr. 2, 93055 Regensburg
Germany
Email: Andres.mueller@toshiba-tro.de

Ploog, Martin, Dr.
Institute of Business Administration, Department of Production
Management, Technical University of Braunschweig
Katharinenstr. 3, 38106 Braunschweig
Germany
E-Mail: m.ploog@tu-bs.de

Schröter, Marcus
Institute of Business Administration, Department of Production
Management, Technical University of Braunschweig
Katharinenstr. 3, 38106 Braunschweig
Germany
E-Mail: marcus.schroeter@tu-bs.de

Sieghart, Till
Conti Temic Microelectronic GmbH, Nürnberg
Sieboldstr. 19, 90411 Nürnberg
Germany
E-Mail: till.sieghart@temic.com

Spengler, Thomas, Prof. Dr.
Institute of Business Administration, Department of Production
Management, Technical University of Braunschweig
Katharinenstr. 3, 38106 Braunschweig
Germany
E-Mail: t.spengler@tu-bs.de

Steinfeldt, Michael
Institute for Ecological Economy Research, Berlin
Potsdamer Str. 105, 10785 Berlin
Germany
Email: michael.steinfeldt@ioew.de

Stölting, Wiebke
Institute of Business Administration, Department of Production
Management, Technical University of Braunschweig
Katharinenstr. 3, 38106 Braunschweig
Germany
E-Mail: w.stoelting@tu-bs.de

Wagner, Bernd, Prof. Dr.
Centre for Further Training and Knowledge Transfer
University of Augsburg
Universitätsstr. 16, 86159 Augsburg
Germany
Email: bernd.wagner@zww.uni-augsburg.de

Printed in the United Kingdom by
Lightning Source UK Ltd., Milton Keynes
137931UK00003B/8/A